100
SIMPLE SECRETS
WHY DOGS
MAKE US HAPPY

Also in this series

100
SIMPLE SECRETS
WHY DOGS
MAKE US HAPPY

THE SCIENCE BEHIND
WHAT DOG LOVERS
ALREADY KNOW

DAVID NIVEN, Ph.D.

HarperSanFrancisco
A Division of HarperCollinsPublishers

"Running Dog" flipbook animation copyright © 2007 Tim Romero, Artie Romero, ARG! Cartoon Animation, www.artie.com.

HarperCollins books may be purchased for educational, business, or sales promotional use. For information please write: Special Markets Department, HarperCollins Publishers, 10 East 53rd Street, New York, NY 10022.

HarperCollins Web site: http://www.harpercollins.com

HarperCollins®, ▄®, and HarperSanFrancisco™
are trademarks of HarperCollins Publishers.

FIRST EDITION

Library of Congress Cataloging-in-Publication Data is available.
ISBN 978–0–06–085882–7
ISBN-10: 0–06–085882–6

07 08 09 10 11 CW 10 9 8 7 6 5 4 3 2 1

To Jack, Ralph, Bear, Snoopy, and Snow

Contents

A Note to Readers

For every copy sold of *100 Simple Secrets Why Dogs Make Us Happy*, the author will make a donation to a dog rescue organization. For more information on dog shelters and dog rescue organizations, please visit www.DavidNiven.com.

Introduction: A Dog and His Person

Jack is part Chihuahua and part mystery.

He was quite tiny when I brought him home from the animal shelter. A week or two later, I remember taking a nap on the couch with Jack lying down on the floor by my side. As I woke up, I began to wonder if I might be coming down with a chest cold. I couldn't quite put my finger on it, but I felt there was some kind of slight heaviness to my chest. When I opened my eyes, I changed my diagnosis—I didn't have a chest cold, I had a Chihuahua sleeping on my chest.

As I write this, Jack is curled up in a dog bed near my desk. It's unusual for him to utilize something that's actually meant for dogs—he generally has more of a taste for sleeping on couches, beds, pillows piled on top of more pillows, and people.

I'm not one to quickly assume human characteristics in a dog, but it's hard to deny that Jack seems to happily live some aspects of his life more like a person than a dog. For instance, dogs generally have a hyper-awareness of and interest in their surroundings, but humans can often be oblivious to anything that isn't of immediately obvious importance to them. On this score, Jack acts human. On walks, Jack and I have inadvertently come within a few feet of a squirrel, a raccoon, a cat, and a possum, and Jack didn't try to chase after them, investigate their scent, or do much of anything. Actually, he didn't notice any of them.

While humans may have a certain fussiness and like things a certain way, dogs don't tend to worry a lot about superficial matters. By

xv

contrast, Jack has a discerning eye for the well-manicured lawn. A tree or a fire hydrant may suffice for others to relieve themselves, but Jack likes the feel of healthy-looking, evenly cut, short grass.

You often hear people say of a small dog that he's "a big dog trapped in a small dog's body." But Jack has no delusions or even apparent aspirations in that area. A strange noise in the middle of the night might prompt a growl or a bark, but he tends to proceed no farther than the doorway. He then turns around to look at me, as if to say, "Why don't you just go ahead and check this one out?"

It was on a visit to my mother's home when I let Jack out to explore a wooded section of her backyard that he first encountered the neighbor's Rottweilers. Unbeknownst to him, they were friendly. But in a split-second, he sized them up and decided this was no time for pleasantries and the formal protocol of dog greetings. Jack took off at full speed. The Rottweilers, up for a little game of chase, obliged with a full-speed pursuit.

Jack ran toward the back door, followed by the Rottweilers, followed by me, followed by Bob, the Rottweilers' owner. This was the door we would normally use to go in and out, but Jack determined that he didn't have enough of a lead on his pursuers. Perhaps he could ditch them on the way to the front door.

He scrambled around the corner of the house, around the cellar doors, and flew from the ground to the front door without pausing to use the steps. He let out perhaps the loudest bark he's ever uttered. My mother let him in as the rest of us converged at the front door. As he happily took refuge in the house, he gave me a look. "What were you thinking?" he seemed to ask.

Though he may have a few human habits and isn't likely to win Watchdog of the Year, these are just amusing quirks of his personality. The important thing is that Jack is an incomparable friend. My life has been far richer for the pleasure of his company.

This book is about Jack and the millions of other dogs who come into our lives and affect how we live and who we are. Based on the best research available, studying the lives of people, dogs, and the intersection of the two, *100 Simple Secrets Why Dogs Make Us Happy* reveals how and why dogs make us happier, healthier, more effective, and more satisfied with our lives.

As he sits here watching me type, I'm sure Jack would be pleased to know how important dogs are to people, even if he's not entirely convinced which one he is.

Today Jack has the look and zeal of a young dog. He loves meeting new people and seems to take it as a compliment that everyone assumes he's a puppy.

When I visited the Franklin County Animal Shelter in Columbus, Ohio, twelve years ago to adopt a dog, the first room I entered had two young dogs. They were in separate large pens. The first dog had massive paws and looked to be on his way to growing up to be the size of a moose. Living in an apartment that did not allow dogs, I thought the moose might make dodging the authorities a little dicey. I stopped to pet the dog and said I was sorry but I was sure someone would be along

soon to take him home. The second was a tiny, long-haired, utterly silly-looking dog. I stuck my finger in the pen—something you're not really supposed to do with a dog you know nothing about. The Chihuahua sized up the offer of a finger—and immediately moved over to lick it.

He looked up at me. "Friends?" Jack seemed to ask.

"Forever," I replied.

Dogs Have Personality

Human personalities are one of the aspects of our existence that make us interesting. We don't all react the same way to the same situation—and that very uniqueness can come to define who we are. In this, we are very much like dogs. Dogs may be feisty or friendly or fearless or phobic, but they are who they are.

WHEN ERICA TOOK her dog Odie in to audition for the "Stupid Pet Tricks" segment on *The David Letterman Show*, the coordinator told her why the show has featured so many dogs and so few cats.

"Dogs have personality," he told her. "They really interact with you and can make a connection. Cats, on the other hand, are pretty much indifferent. It's hard to get a reaction out of them."

That was hardly a problem for Odie. Although Erica has no explanation for it, Odie responds when she says, "I love you, Odie."

Odie barks out a very human-sounding "I ruv you."

It was nothing Erica had taught Odie to do—he just did it.

The trick sparked the interest of the Letterman producers, and Erica and Odie appeared on the show a few weeks later. Odie's bark of love was so amazing that it was later voted one of the most memorable TV moments of the year.

While she doesn't know where this talent came from, Erica knows that Odie loves the attention. "After we'd been on the show, everybody we saw would stop us and talk to Odie. He was in heaven."

Personality tests show that dogs are as likely as humans to demonstrate consistent personality traits. (Gosling, Kwan, and John 2003)

Dogs Provide Visible Love

In many human relationships, our feelings for each other are assumed. We speak of our love and show our love far less than we are capable of because we don't even think about it, or because it's easier or safer to assume that it's understood. But dogs have no hesitation to show their affection. They do not worry about hiding their feelings, and in the process they not only show us that we are appreciated but remind us to share our feelings for those around us—canine or human.

THERE WASN'T A LOT of room for affection in Joe's work. Before shipping home, the Oregon National Guardsman patrolled the streets of Baghdad.

But there was Daisy, a scrawny mutt who hung around the army base. Daisy had made friends with the last unit to occupy the base, and as Joe and the rest of the 162nd Infantry arrived, soldiers asked the new troops to take care of her.

Officially it was against the rules. But no one saw the value of forcing Daisy out into a grim future on the streets of the city.

Soldiers had been slipping Daisy some military rations, but she didn't start to fill out until Joe had his wife ship him a case of dog food.

Daisy meant so much to Joe and his fellow troops that when it was time to return to the United States, Joe wanted Daisy to come home with him. With Daisy unwelcome on a military flight, Joe researched a private carrier that could get Daisy from Iraq to Kuwait and, after several more stops in between, eventually to Oregon.

It was an unusual commitment to make, but Joe had no doubt. "Daisy helped us get through that experience. For everybody in the unit, Daisy was a little bit of love, a little bit of hope in our day," Joe says.

In one study nearly all dog owners said that they could think of an example of their dog showing them affection that day, while only four out of ten could think of an example of a human showing them affection that day. (Roth 2005)

We Feel Better in Minutes

We are always looking for the magic elixir that will make us feel better right now. While that search continues, we already know one thing that will make us feel better in the span of time it takes to walk into a room: spending a moment with a dog. In a matter of minutes, dogs can change our mood and our physical system, making us feel better just to be with them.

LISA'S FOCUS WAS on her career. "It wasn't just while I was at the office that I thought of work first," Lisa says. "Work was a part of every decision I made. Six months after I started I moved twenty minutes closer to the office so that I could spend that extra time working."

But when her company's retail stores saw their sales decline, Lisa's entire department was laid off. At some level she knew it wasn't her fault. It wasn't anything she had done that caused her to lose her job. Still, she didn't really accept that.

"It's hard to take a job loss as anything but a personal failure," she says.

Out of work for the first time in her adult life, and muddling through a bumpy search for a new job, Lisa fell into nearly constant sadness.

Things didn't start to look up until a friend asked a huge favor. Could she take care of Parker, a Gordon setter, while the friend was out of town for three weeks?

Lisa was reluctant. She'd never had a dog—she'd never had the time for one. But she said yes because she didn't want to see the dog sent off to a kennel for that long.

Lisa was amazed at Parker's effect on her life. "There was this whole new vibe to my life," Lisa says. "It's silly, but there was something else on my plate besides worrying about finding a job. And even when I was working on my job search, somehow it didn't seem so hopeless with a big smiling face and wagging tail by my side."

Contact with a dog has positive effects on stress levels and immune functions that start in less than five minutes and endure for more than nine times as long as the contact itself. (Barker et al. 2005)

4

Dogs Are Nonjudgmental

Dogs do not ask us why we didn't get a promotion. They don't ask us why we don't have a bigger house or a new car. They don't ask for anything superficial. Instead, in caring for them, dogs reinforce our basic sense of personal capability and the irrelevance of much of what we compete for.

SARA HAS SOMETHING of an unusual task. Her main job is to sit quietly and listen to children read. Children tell their teachers that Sara really likes it when they read to her. More important, Sara is unlikely to make a face if they stumble over a word. That could be because Sara is a dog.

Sara makes the rounds of Dayton-area elementary schools because teachers have found that young readers do better with an audience, but only an audience that is accepting.

"The worst thing you can do to a child just starting to read is to make them focus strictly on their mistakes," says Alice, a reading teacher. "If children think all anybody is paying attention to is when they mispronounce a word or don't recognize a word, then they will fear reading, and they will try to avoid reading. And then you have a cycle that goes from bad to worse."

Teachers have found that reading to Sara gives children the chance to practice reading familiar stories out loud without feeling bored and to try out new stories without feeling nervous.

"And it's really quite amazing because Sara is as real an audience to them as any group of people would be," Alice says. "But Sara never embarrasses them, never makes them feel uncomfortable. Instead of reading being a threat, Sara helps the children to see it as a joy. And that makes all the difference."

Two groups of people were asked to describe their lives. The first group included dog owners who were with their dogs. The second group was made up of people who did not own a dog. The first group was 14 percent less likely to respond to the question negatively, and 23 percent less likely to complain about their job or salary. (Glucksman 2005)

Dogs Make Us Look Positive

In any given moment, much of how we feel is subjective. There is no objective way to measure our mood, just a tendency to pay attention to certain indicators. Paradoxically, one important contributor to how we feel is how others think we feel. If they conclude that we're happy, we're more likely to be happy. Among their other effects, dogs dramatically increase the likelihood that others will think we're happy.

WINSTON IS A TYPICAL Jack Russell terrier. He's all energy all the time. "He's not the kind of dog you feel comfortable leaving at home for long stretches at a time," says his owner Brent. There might not be much home left when you return.

So Brent, a concert promoter in Denver, started taking Winston to work with him. Winston has now met Paul Simon, the Who, and a host of other famous musicians.

With some obedience school training, Brent was able to at least channel Winston's energy into things like chasing Frisbees. In fact, Winston embraced Frisbees so much that "now we can't even say the word," Brent says. "We have to spell it around him or he goes nuts."

With more training, Winston proved an ace at an array of dog tricks.

When a member of the front office for Denver's hockey team, the Colorado Avalanche, spotted Winston jumping through hoops, he spoke to Brent about making Winston the team's mascot.

Winston took to the job immediately. Wearing a cape in the team colors, Winston has appeared at games and charity events and in team commercials. Everywhere he goes, he gets a huge reaction.

Brent says Winston loves it. "He's always wanted to be in the center of attention." And Brent doesn't mind either. "Everybody likes the guy with the most popular dog in town."

When evaluating others, we are 42 percent more likely to think they are happy if they have a dog with them. (Rossbach and Wilson 1992)

6

Dogs Take Us Walking

Many good habits can be difficult or unpleasant to carry out, but that's certainly not true of all of them. There can be tremendous pleasure in the simple and valuable act of taking a walk, which not only burns calories but decreases stress. Having a dog requires that you regularly take walks—it's something you do for your dog, but in truth your dog is doing it for you.

AS PHYLLIS PUTS IT, "They'd written me off."

Years of medical difficulties had left her bedridden and her overall health in steady decline. But she refused to give in to hopelessness. Slowly she turned the corner toward minimal mobility, then to being able to get around town, and finally she decided to take a walk ... across the state of Kansas.

None of this would have been possible without Justice, Phyllis's dog. With Justice, Phyllis can now walk farther and faster, and she never lacks for a willing companion.

"I wanted to get going, so I got Justice," Phyllis says. "Now I want to keep going, and Justice helps make sure I can and that I do. Dogs don't give up, they keep going. And that's just what I needed in my life.

11

"It's hard for me to believe what my life was once like," Phyllis says. "It was awful. But remembering it gives me appreciation for what I have now."

Dog owners walk 79 percent farther in an average week than those who don't own a dog. (Brown and Rhodes 2006)

Life Is More Enjoyable

When we think of what's important for a satisfying life, we think of family, career, and our most memorable experiences. Add to that list: having a dog. People with a dog are more likely to think positively about themselves and about the world around them, and they are less likely to focus on their fears and disappointments. In direct and indirect ways, people with a dog feel better about their lives.

THEY FACE SOME of the most challenging days anyone could ever have at work. And when they finish a job, they have to be immediately ready for the next one. But the firefighters on the north side of Pittsburgh know that there will be a friendly face waiting for them back at the station.

"A fireman and a dog is kind of a cliché," says Steve, a ten-year veteran of the squad. "But the reason it's such a widely known image is that we really love dogs."

The station's dog is not the Dalmatian one might expect. But Max, a four-year-old Akita, was literally born for the role. Found outside an abandoned house the crew was using for training, Max quickly made a home in the station.

"We take care of him, but he really takes care of us," says Steve. "He helps take the edge off a bad day when we can come back and see him jump on us, run around, and make us feel like we're the best guys around."

Even after factoring in the effects of people's marriage, education, income, age, and gender, having a dog independently increased the likelihood of life satisfaction by 12 percent. (Richang, Na, and Headey 2005)

Dogs Help Us Show Affection

Dogs do more for us than make us happy by showing us affection. They actually change the way we ourselves show affection. We become less reserved around other people and feel better about how we can contribute to our relationships.

SINCE HE WAS a young boy, Troy had been raised by his grandmother. He suffered from the loss of parents who were not an active part of his life. His grandmother, June, and his aunts offered Troy their love, but they always worried that Troy felt like he didn't really belong.

Troy was ten years old when a medium-sized brown mutt showed up in their yard.

Troy took the dog a bowl of water and food.

June was concerned that they might get too attached to a dog they knew nothing about, a dog someone might be looking for that very moment. But she didn't really think that was likely: the dog was so thin, and he attacked the food Troy gave him.

It wasn't long before the life in Troy's face convinced her that the dog might well be just what he needed. Troy named the dog Zo after his favorite basketball player, Alonzo Mourning.

"It was like you flipped a switch," June says. "Troy found something in that dog. Like they were kindred spirits. I think this really became his home when he could share it with Zo."

People with dogs are 10 percent more likely to display their affection for other people than people without dogs. (Dickstein 1998)

We See Dogs as We See Other Humans

When viewing animals, most of us find it very hard to tell them apart. They just look too similar to us to process, categorize, and remember what makes each animal different. Of course, with other humans we can better process differences in appearance, and we invest more of our attention in remembering them, paying particular attention to people's faces. We do the same with dogs. We have no trouble distinguishing the neighbor's dog from a dog we've never seen before, and it's a crucial aspect of our relationship with dogs that we respond to them as individuals instead of as a category of creatures.

EVAN AND MONICA have a story of how they met, but it's really a story of how Monica met Hudson, Evan's dog.

Monica had seen the gorgeous Samoyed several times while she was walking near the beach in Santa Monica. She'd never paid much attention to Hudson's owner, but she kept noticing the distinctive white dog.

One day she was sitting by herself outside a coffee shop, lamenting that she had lost her keys and didn't know how she was going to get back into her apartment.

And then Hudson ambled up beside her and wagged his tail. Monica smiled at the dog and reached out to pet him. For the first time she noticed his handsome owner.

They struck up a conversation in which Monica said she had noticed Evan's beautiful dog many times and Evan said he had noticed Monica.

Phone numbers were traded, and a relationship began, and as Monica says, "It all started because I felt like I knew Hudson."

The same part of the brain is activated when we see a human face as when we see a dog. (Blonder et al. 2004)

Dogs Understand Math

One of the things that enchants us about dogs is our belief that they have a basic understanding of what's going on around them. They seem to pick up on the patterns all around them and then make keen judgments about what is likely to happen next. And as anyone who has ever tried to cut back on dog biscuits has probably figured out, dogs do a pretty good job of counting as well.

ELVIS CAN DO MATH—and not just any kind of math, but calculus. Discovering Elvis's abilities stunned his owner, Tim Pennings, who is a mathematician himself.

Tim was playing fetch with Elvis on a Lake Michigan beach. Tim would toss the ball into the water and then watch Elvis retrieve it.

After repeated throws, Tim noticed a pattern in Elvis's route. He didn't run straight to the water's edge and swim directly to the ball. Nor did he run to the point where the ball was closest to the shore and jump in. Instead, he ran partway to the water and then swam at an angle toward the ball.

Elvis, Tim realized, was instantly calculating the quickest route to the ball.

The quickest route between two points is a basic calculus equation—and Tim set out to confirm what he suspected. After marking Elvis's route to the ball, Tim brought out paper and pencils and a computer;

three hours later, he'd confirmed that Elvis's path was the fastest available way to the ball.

While Elvis might not be able to plot the equation on paper, the irony of the situation was not lost on Tim. "Elvis was making a calculation in a second. It took me hours to come up with the exact same answer."

Tim wrote a paper on Elvis's math abilities, and sometimes he takes Elvis to lectures he gives on the subject. While Tim speaks and writes equations on the board, Elvis snoozes, apparently content that he already knows the answer.

Experiments using dog biscuits showed that dogs respond to their owners more quickly to simple and correct addition (1 biscuit + 1 biscuit = 2 biscuits) than to incorrect addition. (West and Young 2002)

We Truly Live Together

While any pet has an effect on our life, of very few pets can it be said that we truly live together. Most of the animals you could bring into your home, whether cats, birds, turtles, or fish, do pretty much the same thing much of the time whether you are there or not, and you do pretty much the same thing whether they are there or not. This is not the case with dogs. Our presence matters to them, and theirs to us.

ACTRESS KRISTIN DAVIS played Charlotte on the television show *Sex and the City*. One Charlotte story line involved her completely falling for an acquaintance's dog. Charlotte ultimately wound up with the dog, whom she named Elizabeth Taylor.

After the series ended, Davis starred in the movie *The Shaggy Dog*, in which her character's husband finds himself turning into a dog.

People assume that in real life Davis is similar to the characters she plays—a sweet and good-natured person who loves dogs.

And conveniently, in real life, Davis does love dogs.

In fact, in addition to her own dog she is providing a home for four foster dogs from her local animal shelter. But even in caring for shelter dogs, Davis can't get away from her work: the shelter told her the dogs were named Charlotte, Mr. Big, Samantha, and Stanford, all character names from her show.

Working and living with dogs affects her entire schedule and approach to her day. Davis appreciates many things about dogs, but one of the things she loves the most about them is their sincerity.

"About the only genuine reaction you can count on in Hollywood is from your dog," she says.

Dogs have the highest rate of coordinated behaviors with humans of any household pet. (Miller and Lago 1990)

Dogs Learn Words

Dogs develop a working understanding of several dozen words. While they may not be able to follow the plot of a movie, dogs are perfectly capable of getting the gist of what you have to say about food, walks, and precisely who is allowed on the couch.

BEN, AN OLD FRIEND of Tony's from college, was in town for the weekend, and Tony invited him over to his Chicago apartment. The two men sat around reminiscing about college, talking about their jobs, and arguing over all kinds of topics.

With Tony's German shepherd Rogue lying in the corner of the room, eventually the topic worked its way around to whether dogs can understand words.

Tony said, of course they can, there are all kinds of words dogs can obviously learn. Millions of dogs know what "sit" means, he said.

Ben disagreed. Sure dogs respond, he said, but do they really understand the word or are they seeing hand signals and other cues that help them figure out what they want to do?

Eventually Ben agreed that a dog might be able to respond to a few words, but it was probably the human's distinctive tone of voice in speaking each word, not the word itself, that the dog was responding to.

Tony said he thought Ben might be selling dogs short.

Later, after the conversation had worked its way through a dozen other topics, Ben asked Tony if he wanted to take a walk downtown.

Ben issued this invitation in a completely normal, flat tone, human to human, with no hand signals.

Immediately Rogue shot up and started wagging his tail.

At that point, Ben conceded that he might have underestimated dogs.

Dogs can learn up to one hundred words, both by coming to understand their meaning and by excluding other possible meanings. (Markman and Abelev 2004)

13

It's Hard to Be Fussy

At a certain point in every dog owner's life, a favorite pair of shoes, the newspaper, or even a sofa may be lost. Accidents happen, dog hair seems to build up everywhere but on the dog, and some dogs go through a chewing phase. But the life of loving a dog is a constant reminder of the value of love over things—and the value of being adaptable.

"THERE COMES A TIME in a dog owner's life where you have to abandon your commitment to house perfection," Katie says. "That moment comes about two minutes after you get the dog."

But Katie does not throw up her hands in surrender. She is an interior designer with a thriving specialty in making homes pet-friendly.

"I tell dog owners they can absolutely have things very nice," Katie says. "Their home can look good and be functional for people and for dogs. But there's some flexibility required."

While most people put a great deal of thought into determining the right colors for their rooms, Katie tells them to start with the colors of their dog. "You can't make all the hair disappear, but you can at least hide it between cleanings."

For floors, Katie assesses not only dog hair quantities but a dog's traction as well. "With a big dog, you might want to avoid wood floors, which will get scratched up. You might try tile, but you have to be sure it's not too slippery."

But Katie doesn't see working with a family dog as anything of a compromise in her work. "A properly designed interior is not just there to look good, it's there to look good and serve those who live there. Dogs included."

People who do not like dogs are 31 percent less likely to say they can sit still and enjoy themselves when their home is less than orderly. (Stubbs and Cook 1999)

14

A Bond on Many Levels

One of the reasons our relationship with dogs is so strong is that it is not based on any one thing. There is an emotional connection, a social effect, a behavioral routine, and the impact of a strong commitment. All this combines to bring us closer to our dogs than we are or can be with any other animal.

LYNN'S DOG MAGIC is half Jack Russell terrier and half beagle. As a result of this combination, he has an incredible sense of smell and endless energy to run off as far as the smells might lead him.

Lynn's backyard is enclosed by a combination of fences and natural barriers that would keep almost any other dog from pursuing his wanderlust.

But to Magic a fence is something to find a way over or under, and a stream is something to be ignored altogether.

Lynn felt badly about holding Magic back from his instinct to explore. "It feels like I'm denying him the use of his natural gift. It's like taking golf clubs out of the hands of Tiger Woods."

So from time to time Lynn watched and then followed as Magic made his way over or around whatever might have kept him from exploring the next yard, the yard after that, and whatever lay beyond. Magic always made his way back and then stood on the back steps and made it clear he was ready to go inside now.

Still, Lynn was stunned the next summer when Magic made his way out of the yard only to come right back.

"It was like he was saying there's nothing out there nearly as good as what I've got here," Lynn says.

Studies of people and their family dog have revealed that there is no single aspect of their relationship that explains their bond. (Johannson 2000)

15

Dogs Feed Our Creativity

In many ways, our dogs are a constant puzzle. They give clues as to what they are thinking and what they want, but we must interpret them. We're the keepers of their life stories, but we have to fill in the blanks in those stories. In encouraging us to take creative notice of them, dogs keep us looking creatively at the world.

IT'S NOT PARTICULARLY surprising that Doggy Style Designs, a Rhode Island company that makes items for the pampered pooch, would allow dogs to come to work with their owners. Owner Jeff Gellman's employees can share their workspace with their dogs and take advantage of a kennel and dog run in the company's backyard.

What is surprising to Jeff is that the policy pays dividends not just for the dogs but also for the bottom line.

"This is just tremendous for stress reduction," Jeff says. "People feel more comfortable while they're working. And if they need to take a break, ten minutes out back tossing a ball to their dog gives them a whole new outlook."

And for Jeff that can make all the difference. "Good ideas don't tend to come from people who feel like they're about to burst," he says. "The only thing you can think of in that situation is escape.

"Good ideas come from people who feel supported and appreciated—and dogs help us to feel that. And employers who allow dogs get the benefits."

Jeff sees the effect on himself. "Dogs make me happy—and when I'm happy I'm better at my job."

In a laboratory experiment, people with dogs used 7 percent more strategies when confronted with a problem. (Arambasic et al. 2000)

16

Dogs Are Not Sore Losers

Imagine a competitor who goes all out in the game and, win or lose, is happy when it's over and looks forward to the next chance to play. Sounds unheard of in our hypercompetitive culture, where no loss, however trivial, can be accepted. But dogs play for fun, and they have fun, win or lose.

OVER THE COURSE of more than two decades, Matt has been an umpire for Little League, high school, and college baseball games. It's a hobby he enjoys because he loves baseball and he loves testing himself to maintain the concentration to call a game properly.

More times than he can count, Matt has had to deal with a player who couldn't stand making an out or losing the game. "I look at them, and I think, 'This is fun. There will come a time in your life when you won't get to spend the better part of the day surrounded by friends, playing a game.'"

But Matt knows that's not how most players see it. "This isn't the World Series or anything. These players don't have million-dollar contracts," Matt says, "but anything other than success is unacceptable."

It's always refreshing for Matt to see a group of kids play the game because they simply enjoy it—and who accept that baseball is a game where even the best make outs far more often than they get hits.

It's the kind of attitude Matt's dog Hank has about sports. While he doesn't hit for average, Hank can field tennis balls that Matt hits to him with a baseball bat. "And the best part is, whether Hank catches it or has to run after it, either way he's happy."

In a series of tug-of-war games between humans and dogs, the dogs were more obedient and attentive after playing than before, regardless of whether they won or lost. (Rooney 2002)

17

Dogs Star in Our Stories

It's not just in old movies and television shows that dogs play a starring role. For children who grow up around dogs, dogs are often among the most compelling characters in the stories they create. The central role of dogs in our imagination illustrates how important they are in how we see and understand the world—and how we see and understand ourselves.

THE MUSICAL *Annie* is the story of an orphaned girl and her stray dog Sandy who find their way into the life of a tycoon who eventually takes them both in.

When the Omaha Community Playhouse staged the play, it held open auditions for actors, both human and dog.

The dog who won the role of Sandy had really lived the part. Her owners found her in an area animal shelter, where she had been taken after being found stray on the streets.

While Annie is the star of the show, director Susan Collins thinks the story wouldn't work without Sandy.

"Sandy is a key reason why this can be a story about hope even in what is at first a hopeless situation," Susan says.

"Sandy brings love into the story and really provides Annie an outlet for expressing her dreams. After all, the most remembered part of the show is Annie singing about 'Tomorrow,' and she's singing to Sandy."

In a study of Chinese, Hungarian, and Swedish children's stories featuring dogs as characters, 87 percent were portrayed in positive, usually playful terms. (Carlsson et al. 2001)

18

Having a Dog Is Like Parenting Without the Diapers

Dogs trigger a reaction in us that's similar to the parenting instinct we have toward infants and toddlers. We think about the needs of dogs, we protect them from danger, and we try to make them happy. In carrying out our responsibility for our own dog's welfare, we gain the joy of that responsibility.

COLLEEN FEELS it herself, but seeing it in her grade school–aged son and daughter is even more of a joy. It's the parenting instinct—to take care of and protect their part-poodle part-unknown little dog Marvin.

"I remember the connection I felt to Lucky, my first dog, when I was little," Colleen says. "It was really the first time I realized I could be useful to somebody. When you are that age, you are used to relying on others, but nobody relies on you. But when I let Lucky out, when I got her a dog biscuit, it was me in the grown-up role."

Today Colleen sees her children doing the exact same thing. "They will pout if the other one gets to feed Marvin. And when they have friends over, they start a lecture on the best way to pet Marvin," she says.

"Marvin is the kind of dog who always wants to be around you, and we all respond to that. We want to be around him, to see his tail wag all day long," Colleen says. "You don't really think parenting skills are something an eight-year-old and a forty-year-old have in common, but with Marvin it is."

Observed with their dogs, 84 percent of people displayed elements of parental behavior. (Prato-Previde, Fallani, and Valsecchi 2006)

19

We Connect Through Our Eyes

From an early age, we learn to communicate with our eyes. Being able to see someone's eyes as we speak not only confirms that attention is being paid but establishes an emotional connection as well. Dogs look to our eyes to help communicate with us just as humans do.

KATIE IS AN EXCELLENT judge of the power of eye contact in communicating with her dog Satchel. Satchel, a boxer, is deaf, but Katie has no trouble getting her point across.

The biggest challenge, Katie says, is getting over automatic reactions. "We all have a natural inclination to say no when something is wrong," Katie says. "But with Satchel, that's useless."

With a combination of her hands and her eyes, though, Katie can be understood.

When Satchel made a grab for the family's dinner one time, just the force of a disapproving eye sent him scurrying out of the room.

Satchel has been trained to recognize hand signals for the usual "sit" and "stay" signals as well as for "good boy."

Her experience with Satchel has taught Katie how much more there is to communication than sound. "Dogs communicate with each other with a lot of body language," Katie says, "and between our hands and our eyes, there is a lot we are telling dogs."

In an experiment, dogs were 44 percent less likely to approach a human whose eyes were closed or blindfolded than a human whose eyes were open. (Gácsi et al. 2004)

20

Our Homes Feel More Like a Home

A home begins as nothing more than physical space—walls, floors, furniture. For a home to be an emotionally welcoming place, it must contain more than space and stuff. It must be filled with love. Having a dog changes a home in more ways than just the scattered bits of dog hair—it becomes a shared place of commitment and caring and a base of support and affection.

AS A REAL ESTATE agent, Al has a pretty developed sense of the difference between a house and a home.

"A house only needs to be functional," Al says. "But a home is almost a living thing. You might feel comfortable in a hotel room, for example, but you never feel at home. It functions, but it has nothing to do with your life, with who you are."

While it's a little harder for a real estate agent to show a house with a dog—you have to either make sure the dog doesn't sneak out while you're there or arrange to have the dog be out of the house, and there's always the possibility that the dog will pick that day to have an accident—still, Al feels that a house with a dog is a much easier place for a buyer to imagine as his or her home.

"When you see the dog there, you just get this whole sense of what goes on in this place," Al says. "This is not just a warehouse to hold somebody's clothing. It's a place where there's life and love."

Looking at pictures of the inside of a house, college students were 48 percent more likely to think it was a loving home if there was a dog in the picture. (Wells and Perrine 2001)

21

We Look on the Bright Side

Dogs offer a powerful lesson in basic optimism. Dogs look forward to your coming home. Dogs look forward to dinner. Dogs look forward to a walk. Dogs embrace what they like and seek it. And no dog pauses in the middle of a meal or a long walk to worry about what comes next.

"RETIREMENT TAKES SOME figuring out," says Sam. "You have a lot of free time, but how are you going to spend it? You would think a person with lots of free time wouldn't have any worries. But what you really have is more time to worry."

Sam's retired friends spend a lot of time wondering about their health and their finances. "We sit around and somebody will always come up with something new to get worked up about."

But Sam tries to follow the approach of Scout, his Shar-Pei.

Shar-Peis have wrinkled skin that looks like a suit desperately in need of an iron. "Does Scout stop to worry about why he looks different from all the other dogs on the block?" Sam asks. "No, it doesn't seem to bother him one bit.

"Scout has a good day today. Then he has a good day tomorrow. He's happy when we go for a walk in the morning, happy when we stop and visit people, and happy when we get back home," Sam says.

"He gets enjoyment out of what he does, and then does it again. There's a lot of smart people I know who can't say the same."

Dog owners are 14 percent more likely to be optimistic about their day than nondog owners. (Collins 2005)

22

We Understand Their Language

Describe the sound of a dog barking. You might first think of it as just a noise, an indecipherable sound that carries no particular message, like the whine of a lawn mower or the pounding of a hammer. But when you really stop to consider it, think about how much a dog conveys with a bark. The bark of alarm is very different from the bark of an excited hello. We decode the messages of dogs far better than we think we do.

RAY IS A SPEECH therapist. He spends his days helping grade-school children form the sounds that make up words. He pays close attention to their every sound, listening for the differences and watching the techniques of forming sound.

And while Ray is less hopeful that Barkley will learn to say words, he's listened closely to the sound of his dog as well. "I know he cannot talk," Ray says of his Weimaraner. "But it sure seems like he has something to say."

Out of curiosity, Ray has tape-recorded examples of Barkley's barks. He says that the difference between Barkley's alarm when a delivery man knocks on the door and the happy sound he makes when Ray says it's time for a walk is particularly distinct.

"There is a pitch and rhythm to barking that is very clear if you listen for it," Ray says. "And when you combine that with the body language when barking, the differences are even more clear."

Scientists testing people's ability to understand dog barking played recordings of barking and asked them to guess the situation that the dog was in. Listeners correctly classified the dog's situation more than seven out of ten times, suggesting that dogs are really talking to us in their barking. (Pongrácz et al. 2005a)

23

We're Less Likely to Be Ignored

Dogs attract attention and comment. There is something inviting about the people you see out in public with a dog—they seem to have interests beyond themselves and an openness with others. Being in public with a dog invites interaction in a way that being out by yourself does not.

WILL WAS IN A North Carolina animal shelter, in the process of adopting a husky named Rocky. While he was there, he noticed Krista, a volunteer at the shelter.

They fell easily into conversation about the shelter, Will's new dog, and themselves. Will left with a dog and a date for Saturday.

"She seemed so nice and sincere," he says. "I liked that she volunteered at the shelter. It's such an unselfish thing to do."

Krista was immediately taken with Will as well. "He was obviously an animal lover. To me, animal lovers are nurturing and caring people, more stable, more responsible," she says. "They often will put others' needs before their own."

While the animal shelter is not exactly advertised as a place to meet new people, Will and Krista are grateful for the opportunity it provided.

Two years after they met there, they were married and living happily with Rocky.

People were two times more likely to speak to a person walking by with a dog than a person walking by carrying an object or nothing at all. (Wells 2004)

24

Dogs Keep Us Calmer

When we are alarmed, our physiology changes. Our bodies respond to threat with a surge of adrenaline and an increased heart rate. This is a natural process and a survival tool. But it is meant for extraordinary circumstances. We cannot function well when we are constantly in a state of alarm. The calming presence of a dog decreases the likelihood that we will feel threatened as well as the length of time we subject ourselves to these stressful responses.

KATHY IS A NURSE who has studied the effects of dogs on humans.

"There is a clear and undeniable effect," Kathy says. "We can show this by people's own ratings of their feelings, but what's more, we can see it on the monitors."

One study Kathy ran showed that hospital patients visited by a human actually had a modest increase in stress levels, while patients visited by a dog became much calmer.

"It's not that dogs are going to cure people of everything that ails them," Kathy says. "But the body is not built for constant stress. Stress literally breaks down our most fundamental defenses, our immune system. Dogs help promote a healthy system, which in the long run will keep us feeling better than we would without them."

While she doesn't hook herself up to a heart monitor, Kathy knows from personal experience what a dog can do. "There's nothing more

comforting when I get home from the hospital than to see Laddie wagging his tail at me when I come in the door."

With their dogs, people are 34 percent less likely to experience an increased heart rate or other signs of stress responses. (Lefkowitz 2005)

25

Dogs Teach Us Valuable Lessons

There may be no task more important for parents than imparting lessons about values to their children. Dogs offer a wonderful means—every single day—to teach basic lessons about concern for others, the meaning of commitment and responsibility, and the joy of our closest connections in life.

ANGELA'S TEENAGE DAUGHTER Chloe is so calm and compassionate as she cares for their Chihuahua Pedro that at times it has brought a tear to Angela's eyes.

Chloe has diabetes. And Pedro does too.

Pedro requires twice-a-day insulin shots, which more often than not Chloe applies. Chloe herself has received insulin shots since she was in kindergarten—in fact, she learned to inject herself soon after her diagnosis.

Chloe is an expert in the method: she warms the insulin in her hand before injecting it because it stings less that way, and she tries to find the least painful scruff of skin available for the shot. She speaks soothingly to Pedro and rubs him gently.

While Angela marvels at her daughter's ability to persevere through her own health challenges—having to be careful about everything she eats and continually monitor her blood sugar—Chloe gives Pedro credit for the example she sets.

"He's such a good little dog," Chloe says. "He doesn't know why he has to get poked all the time, but he accepts it from me, and he doesn't even know we have this in common. I wish I could make it all better for him, but at least I can help keep him as healthy as possible."

Children raised with dogs in the home are 9 percent more likely to be kind to others. (Bierer 2001)

26

Do You Have a Dog Lover's Personality? Yes

Who would make a better dog owner—a creative person such as an artist or a more buttoned-down person such as an accountant? Who would make a better dog owner—a person who cares for a large family or a person living alone? The answer is that attachment to dogs is unrelated to our personality type or living situation. Anybody can love a dog.

NATALIE DIDN'T START out with dogs in her life.

"My mother was a cat person, so I really only had cats in my life growing up," she says.

To Natalie, having cats was part of her identity. "It's so much a part of your life. The rhythms of caring for a pet are so different for a cat than a dog. Your responsibilities and expectations are so different. It all seemed to fit me so well."

While Natalie had nothing against dogs, she couldn't forget her friends' stories about their dogs that ate sofas, tore through screen porches, and knocked over everything in sight.

But after a lifetime with cats, Natalie developed allergies. "Suddenly you have to reexamine all your pet assumptions. You can't have a cat, and you've never really thought of a life with a dog before."

Determined not to face an empty house as her youngest daughter was preparing to leave for college, Natalie decided it was time to find a dog.

Her friends were stunned when they found she had adopted a little Welsh corgi named Bobby. They asked what she was doing, since she wasn't a dog person. And she quickly found out the answer.

"It turns out I am," Natalie says.

Attachment to dogs is not dependent on human personality type. (Bagley and Gonsman 2005)

27

Dogs Make Us Feel Vital

W̲e̲ all have a fundamental need to feel capable. We must know that there are important things that need to be done and that we can do them. Providing for a dog is a tangible reminder of what we can do, and what we must do, to care for another.

LENORE IS EIGHTY-FIVE years old. She's been a widow for more than two decades. And yet she bounds out of the house each day with a smile. Her neighbors, less than half her age, marvel at her energy.

Lenore gives a lot of the credit to Socrates, who is the reason she's up and out as early as she is. Lenore says that Socrates, a Norwich terrier, is "not afraid to nudge you when he thinks it's time to go out. Sometimes I wonder if he's part rooster."

Still, Lenore says, "Socrates is the treasure of my life."

Lenore values not just the companionship of Socrates but also the sense of purpose he helps provide. "Caring for someone—two-legged or four-legged—is a natural part of life," she says. "It makes you feel needed."

When Lenore was talking about getting a dog, her children tried to talk her out it. "They suggested I might be too old to get a dog. But I think I might be too old not to have one."

Middle-aged women who owned a dog were 10 percent less likely to define their abilities by their age. (Downey 2002)

28

A Much Needed Source of Consistency

So much of daily life is uncertain. A bad day at work, a traffic jam, or an unpleasant trip to the store can send us spiraling off into a grumpy view of our day or even ourselves. But our dogs don't have bad days. They don't decide they are too busy to pay attention to us today. Dogs provide a constant in life, which has almost no certainties.

MICHAEL WORKS IN SALES. His salary and his prospects for advancement depend on the decisions of customers; he can try to influence these decisions using every technique available to him, but ultimately they are somebody else's to make. When Michael goes into work, he has no idea if he will leave feeling spectacularly successful, average, or a complete failure.

Michael has heard it said more than once, "If you want a friend in this business, get a dog." A firm believer in this bit of wisdom, he has a dog, a Great Dane named Duffy.

For Michael, Duffy represents almost the opposite of everything in his work life.

"Sales is a constant battle against cynicism," Michael says. "People assume you are trying to take advantage of them, and you have to assume they're trying to take advantage of you."

Duffy, on the other hand, never seems to doubt Michael's motives. "Dogs are congenitally trusting and forgiving," Michael says.

And for Michael, very important, you know what to expect with a dog. "Anything could happen at work, but when I get home, there will be big, slobbering, tail-wagging Duffy, happy to see me, and waiting for a nice long walk and some scratching behind the ears."

For eight out of ten dog owners, their dog rates among the three most reliable and consistent aspects of their lives. (Mueller 2003)

29

We Think They're Human

While dogs and humans have much in common, one source of our fascination with dogs is our exaggeration of how much we and they have in common. We imagine so many human traits in dogs and delight in them—even when they're not there.

TERRY KNOWS IT'S SILLY. Her dog Baby isn't human. Sure she recognizes some words and gets the gist of what Terry is trying to tell her, but she can't really follow her stories about work and her friends and world events. *Still ...*

Baby's qualities are so often similar to those of humans.

Baby is as relentless as a child when Terry is slow to toss her a treat after a walk.

Baby is as alert as a seasoned navigator when they drive home from a weekend out of town and appears to recognize the neighborhood even when Terry takes a route from an unfamiliar direction.

Baby is as kind as a loved one when Terry is down.

"When I've had a bad day, Baby comforts me. She may not understand exactly what happened, but what's more important, understanding the details of a bad day at work or caring?"

In that respect, Terry says that maybe Baby doesn't sound human. "Not that many humans I know are that nice."

Dogs are 50 percent more likely to be portrayed with human qualities and abilities in *New Yorker* cartoons today than they were eighty years ago. (Alden 2004)

30

Dogs Pay Attention to Us

In a day filled with tasks, and in our culture built on independence, it's not hard to go a day or even a few days without having a real conversation with someone. Many of us could easily develop feelings of isolation by the end of an average day. The dog in our lives, however, will pay attention to us. Our dog wants to see us and interact with us. It's hard to spend time with your dog and feel disconnected.

SAM MORGAN IS A SOCIOLOGIST who studies human interactions. A lot of what he's learned is visible in his own life.

Growing up, Sam could not set foot outside his front door without seeing a half-dozen people who knew him by name. Now Sam knows a grand total of one neighbor.

"It's just a fact of the times," Sam says. "People are less likely to feel connected to the people who live around them. We've replaced the kinds of interactions that used to be automatic with the kinds of interactions that require an active choice."

In other words, when you are close to a neighbor, you will see that person often and on a spontaneous basis. But relationships with other friends take effort, and without planned meetings you might see them only rarely.

"More and more people feel isolated, because a lot of people will spend a lot less time in each other's company these days," Sam says. "And because there is less room for chance to bring them together."

Both in his own life and in his research, Sam has seen that dogs reduce the likelihood of isolation. "Not only do you have the relationship with the dog, but the dog tends to force you outside where you will have more interactions with other people," Sam says.

By simply paying attention to their owners and fostering positive interactions, dogs reduce the chance of their owner feeling isolated by 21 percent. (Odendaal 2001)

31

Dogs Transcend Our Categories

When we find out a person's age or job or income or marital status, we automatically make all kinds of assumptions about that person's personality, habits, and likes and dislikes. But love for dogs crosses all these boundaries, providing a point of common interest for people who just might not have anything else in common.

A GROUP OF New York–area pug owners gathers once a week in Bronx River Park for a collective pug walk. Their mile-long walk along the river includes stops for marking trees, drinks of water, and dog treats. The pug is an unusual-looking dog: short with a large head and rumpled face, thick neck, and broad shoulders, it has a fire hydrant of a body. On this walk all the dogs may look alike, but their owners could hardly be more different.

Everyone in the group has a pug, but they have little else in common. "People come in from all different places," says Cam, who helped to start the pug walk. "Some are in the city. Some are way out in the suburbs. We have office workers, blue-collar workers, lawyers, and retirees.

"But it doesn't matter who you are—as long as you have a pug, you're welcome," Cam says.

Conversations during the walks reflect their common interest. "We don't talk about work or that kind of stuff," Cam says. "We talk about the dogs for the most part."

Pugs, he says, "are a lot of dog in a little package." Their owners may be "a little different, but they're very loyal."

Attachment to dogs is very strong across demographic traits and is less related to one's characteristics than is true of attachment to cats and other kinds of pets. (Bagley and Gonsman 2005)

32

Dogs Really Are Happy to See Us

We walk in the door and see the tail-wagging excitement of our dog, who seems so eager to see us. We imagine there is no one in the world our dog would rather see. And the fact of the matter is that there really isn't anybody else our dog would rather see.

WHEN LAURA AND KEN return home from work, there is little they look forward to more than seeing the dance of happiness their dog Molly starts as soon as she sees one of them.

"She does this thing—it's a little jump, then a twirl-around, then another little jump—we call it the dance of happiness."

Molly, a French bulldog with an intimidating facial expression but a friendly disposition, leads a pretty comfortable life. "We joke and ask her if she wants to stay outside longer," Laura says. "But after a walk she's looking for a nap on her favorite pillow."

In the commotion of moving into a new house—they had the door and the gate to the fence open as they carried in boxes and furniture—Laura thought Ken was keeping an eye on Molly. And Ken thought Laura was keeping an eye on Molly. It took awhile for them to realize that Molly wasn't with either of them.

At first they were calm, imagining that Molly might have picked out a quiet closet for a nap. But she was nowhere to be found in the house. And she was not in the yard. They scoured the yards of nearby houses and asked if anyone had seen her.

No one had. Laura and Ken searched the area and posted notices everywhere they could.

One harrowing week later, a man five miles away saw Molly in his backyard. She had the look of a lost pet. Fortunately, Molly also has an ID tag on her collar.

The good Samaritan gave Molly food and water and tracked down Laura and Ken.

Though she was filthy and undernourished, Molly did the dance of happiness the moment Laura and Ken came into sight. And Laura and Ken cried from the joy of seeing their dog again.

In a study, dogs left alone were greeted by either their owner or a stranger. Upon returning to the dog, owners were greeted for 38 percent longer than strangers and were 52 percent more likely to be greeted with tail wagging. (Prato-Previde et al. 2003)

33

Dogs Teach Teamwork

L ife with a dog is a constant lesson in teamwork. Two creatures with different abilities and perspectives have to learn enough about each other to function together. These lessons have applications beyond taking walks and learning not to jump on strangers—they reinforce the fundamental ability to successfully coexist with another.

HEATHER, A PROFESSIONAL dog trainer, is committed to her work. But, she says, there is a difference between being serious *about* training a dog and being serious *while* training a dog.

"Dog owners want this to work so badly that they forget how much better it would be, for them and their dog, to have a little fun in the process," she says. "They wind up serious about the task, serious about giving negative feedback, and even serious while praising the dog for doing something good."

Heather says that people who come to her wanting to break their dog of a bad habit are all too used to thinking that a loud, angry voice is the path to success. Even though if a loud, angry voice had been effective, then they wouldn't need Heather.

"This isn't boot camp. The more anxious and overreactive you are, the harder it will be for your dog to learn." That's why Heather requires smiles and laughter on the part of her dog owners.

"Training a dog to work with us includes training ourselves to work with a dog," she says. To get her human pupils in the right frame of

mind, Heather's first lesson includes having them get down on all fours to start seeing things from their dog's perspective.

"When people start to laugh at the situation instead of fume about it, then they're ready to really start working productively with their dog."

After a classroom experience in training dogs, seven in ten students were rated as improved in their ability to work with other students. (Siegel 1999)

34

Dogs Affect Us More Than Cats Do

D og people don't quite understand cat people. In the eyes of a dog person, instead of the boundless enthusiasm of dogs, cats offer indifference. While everyone is entitled to their preferences, the truth is that cats do really have less influence on us and, more important, less positive influence on us.

ACCOMMODATING HER CHILDREN'S wishes, Linda has had experience with cats, hamsters, fish, and a handful of other creatures. But what she really thinks about all these animals is that there isn't anything better than a dog. "Dogs have families, and cats have staff," Linda says.

Growing up the only girl in a family full of brothers, she had doubts that anyone in her house understood her other than her dog Pepper.

While her brothers always had something else to do, and no, she could not come along, Linda and Pepper would go on very long walks, exploring on summer afternoons.

When no one else seemed interested in her math homework or her reading assignment, Pepper would happily sit next to her as she worked.

Every time the subject of a pet came up, Linda was skeptical about her children's newfound interest. Eventually she would give in. But after a brief period of excitement, an unstated reality would sink in: it's hard to really be friends with a hamster.

"You can bring a pet into your home," Linda says, "but for the most part they're there to live their life, not to let you share in their life and to share in yours."

Eventually Linda turned family opinion in the direction of a dog, and when they got one, "for once the thrill of a new pet never went away."

While there is a significant long-term effect of dogs on our health, cats have no effect on us. (Friedmann and Thomas 1998)

35

We Believe in Ourselves More

How we feel about ourselves is a complicated calculation based on how we see ourselves and how we think others see us. Having a dog increases the likelihood that we will see the positive qualities in ourselves, in part because we see those qualities come out as we care for our dog, and in part because they are reflected back to us in our dog's reaction.

THERESA KNOWS THERE are countless summer camps to which parents can send their children. All parents hope to find a camp that will give their child a positive experience, something unique that the child can't get in everyday life.

So why does Theresa's camp ask parents to send not only their children but also their dogs? "A kid with a dog is a happy kid," she says. "It's proven time and time again."

Theresa's camp teaches the children to teach their dogs basic obedience skills. Theresa says the biggest hurdle for most people—adults and children—is that they don't know how to show their dog what they want done. "Your whole focus has to be on communicating—not just your words and your tone, but your body language."

Campers leave amazed at their ability to get their dog to respond in ways they'd never seen before.

But from Theresa's perspective, there is something more going on than a lot of sitting and staying on command. "Both the children and

dogs learn from the experience," Theresa says, "but a big part of the joy of this is seeing the children's confidence and self-esteem grow as they see the effects they can have."

Grade-school students with a dog are 11 percent more likely to have positive self-esteem than students who do not have a dog. (Bierer 2001)

36

Dogs Ask, "Are You Talking to Me?"

Dogs pay attention not only to what we are saying but to whom we are speaking. They understand that even the same word spoken in the same tone is meant for someone else if we are speaking in that person's direction.

WHILE HE HAD had dogs before in his life, Herb had never been the primary caregiver, the one who taught the basic lessons and took care of the dog on a daily basis.

When Herb was retired and living alone, his daughter brought him a dog because she thought it might do her father and the dog, a terrier mix, some good.

Herb housetrained Champ and taught him a few basic tricks and the rules of the house, including not getting up on the furniture.

Herb was impressed with how Champ paid attention to what he was asked to do and how quickly he adapted to his new home. And even when Herb watched the ball game on TV, with Champ at his feet, Champ never seemed to take it personally when Herb would yell at the umpire.

It was more than strange, then, when Herb woke up in the middle of the night to find Champ standing on him. Champ was very good about staying off the furniture and had never jumped up on the bed like this before. Herb wondered if something might be wrong. He got up and found that a fire had started in the basement of his house.

Herb was able to extinguish the fire without major damage. As he sees it, he owes not only his house but his life to Champ and their ability to communicate with each other.

In one study, dogs responded quite differently to the same word commands from their owner depending on whether the owner was facing the dog, facing down, or facing another person. (Virányi et al. 2004)

37

We Enjoy Other People More

Dog owners tend to live less isolated lives. They see the value of companionship and are better able to identify the good in others. Being open to others makes their lives fuller and the challenges they face less overwhelming.

THERE'S NO QUESTION that some people thought she was a little crazy, but for Maggie there was no doubt that in addition to two hundred human guests, her dog Wilbur would be at her wedding. In fact, he was the best man.

"Wilbur should be there because he's so much a part of my life," Maggie says. "But also because he's the connection that brought a lot of these people into my life."

After years of regular trips to the dog park, Maggie had made more than a half-dozen close friends chatting away as Wilbur and the other dogs romped.

And then there's the fact that one of the first things that endeared Maggie's future husband to her was how he responded to Wilbur. "Kyle was great with Wilbur from the first moment," Maggie says. "Wilbur would bound over to him, and Kyle would mess around with him a little bit.

"Sure it seems a little different, but I couldn't quite imagine doing this without Wilbur," she says.

People who grew up with a dog are 31 percent less likely to say they sometimes attempt to avoid being around other humans. (Vizek-Vidovic et al. 2001)

38

Dogs Can Do Geometry

Anyone catching something on the fly—whether an outfielder catching a fly ball or a dog catching a Frisbee—knows that the best strategy is to estimate the object's landing point and run in a straight line from your starting position to the landing point. This calculation has to be done almost instantaneously. It turns out that the reason dogs can catch Frisbees is that they can perform this geometric calculation just as humans do.

SKYLER IS A Border collie with a great talent for catching Frisbees.

Skyler's owner, Mark, said that Skyler's ability is a tribute to his focus and intensity.

"To catch a Frisbee, you have to be thinking and acting all in one step," Mark says. "You have to maintain not just an awareness but a predictive awareness of where the Frisbee is going, how fast, where you are, and how fast you need to go to get to the spot it's going at the moment it gets there."

Mark and Skyler have spent countless afternoons in open fields with a Frisbee. "Skyler loves the chase—it's the Border collie in him," Mark says. "Instead of controlling a herd, which takes all kinds of planning and intensity, actions and reactions, he's focused on controlling what happens to the disc."

Occasionally Mark takes his Frisbee out and tosses it to one of his friends. And when he does, there's no doubt about one thing: "Skyler's

better at catching it. Most of my friends will miss the really long ones because they take a kind of roundabout way to getting where it's going."

Scientists have videotaped the catching process and found that dogs use the same technique to track an object that baseball players use tracking a ball. (Shaffer et al. 2004)

39

When Times Are Tough, Dogs Are There

When something unfortunate happens to us, we need support from those around us. Unfortunately, many people in our lives are afraid to offer support because they know they lack easy answers to our problem. Others are afraid to ask how they can help because they do not want to impose themselves on us. Our relationship with our dog, however, suffers from none of these limitations. We actually feel even closer to our dogs when we are in need, and our dogs are only too happy to respond to our need with their attention and affection.

WHEN JESSICA LOST her husband, it was very hard for her to find comfort from her family and friends. "They didn't know what I needed," she says. "I didn't know what to tell them."

She didn't feel very comfortable talking about her own feelings, and she felt even less comfortable talking about her late husband. But that's what people would ask her about.

Jessica's dog Corky, however, never asked any questions. "He would just come over to me, put his head in my lap, and be with me. I would pet him for hours."

Corky seemed to understand that Jessica was in pain. "He didn't jump around and dance when I came home. But he'd wag his tail and come close to me."

For Jessica, it was exactly what she most needed. "Corky was a tremendous comfort to me and helped me get back to a place where I could more easily welcome others back into my life."

People experiencing a high-stress event were 33 percent more likely to describe their attachment to their dog as high. (Keil 1998)

40

Dogs Fit All Ages

Our lives are transitory: most everything we enjoyed when we were five is no longer of interest to us when we are fifteen, or thirty-five, or eighty-five. But dogs are a source of undiminishing joy. There is comfort in the companionship of a dog whether you have not yet started kindergarten or have been retired for thirty years.

ERNIE KNOWS THAT the lives of his grandchildren are very different from his. Everything they're interested in, from computers to music, is a mystery to him.

But one thing he knows they all have in common is a love for dogs.

Ernie has had dogs since he was a small boy. Raising his family on a farm, he witnessed his loyal dog Blackie get in the way of a mishap waiting to happen when his son was on a collision course with a skunk. And when his young daughter wandered off, it was Blackie who found her and brought her home.

When Ernie bought his two grandchildren a puppy, he saw a look of pure joy on their faces unlike anything he'd seen before. He wondered what kind of adventures they would have together. And he thought that while so much has changed since he was their age, some things are exactly as he remembers them.

"By the time my grandchildren have grandchildren," Ernie says, "the computer will have been replaced by something better, but a dog never will."

High levels of attachment to dogs are found in all age groups, from very young children to people in their nineties. (Downey 2001)

41

Dogs Know Our Mood

For many of us, expressing what we're feeling is a challenge. We lack the words, or we fear that sharing our mood will place an unwelcome burden on others. But dogs don't need for us to explain when we're sad or anxious. Dogs can detect the physiological changes that accompany our feelings—and they respond. Dogs don't need to be asked to pay attention to us, and they don't need to be asked to try to raise our spirits—they're already working on it.

AS A FULL-TIME social worker and part-time dog trainer, Chris is in a unique position to observe the effect of dogs on people's lives.

"In every life there is stress," Chris says. "There is simply no way to avoid that fact. Dogs don't cure the pressures of life, but they can help us deal with those pressures.

"When you are in need, your dog is there for you," Chris says. "You're less likely to feel overwhelmed. Less likely to feel like you should give up."

Chris sees the enormous value in the mundane task of going for a walk. "When you are down, your dog is likely to want to get you going. Going for a walk is a refreshing break from whatever else you were doing or thinking about."

Even when people are very busy, a few moments with their dog can help. Chris points out that "even just a minute spent focusing on your dog—a little scratch behind the ears or rubbing their belly—is a little boost to your well-being and your outlook."

Researchers report that dogs' ability to sense pheromone changes actually improves the ability of therapists to understand their patients' moods. (Anderson 2005)

42

In Dogs We See What We Want to Be

Dogs are confident, strong, loyal, and supportive. In many ways, dogs embody the qualities we hope to see in ourselves.

WHEN BRENDA FIRST brought home Scooter, a Welsh corgi, she had a lot of second thoughts. She had never been personally responsible for a dog before, and she wasn't quite sure she was cut out for it. And, she says, "I failed to react with proper alarm to the words, 'He still needs some work on housetraining.'"

Still, Brenda and Scooter quickly adapted to each other: Scooter learned the importance of not going in the house, and Brenda learned the importance of a very long walk before and after work.

But Brenda sees much more in her relationship with Scooter than accommodation of each other.

"He is always happy to see me," she says. "I have very close friends I can't say that of. He's ready to defend the home and me—although the threats are limited to squirrels and the occasional delivery man. And when I have a bad day at the office, he's never once told me it was my fault."

Brenda wishes we could learn a lesson from Scooter. "I often think how different the world would be if people treated each other more like dogs treat us."

Eighty-eight percent of people surveyed said that their dog had a trait they wished they had themselves. (Glucksman 2005)

43

Dogs Help Keep Us Out of a Rut

As we go through our day, we rarely stop to question much of what we do. As a result, we can overuse something that might be enjoyable or useful in small quantities and turn it into a drain on our lives. Having a dog around makes us less likely to fall into this pattern of behavior, not only because dogs tend to demand our attention when they see us just sitting around, but also because their presence lends variety to our daily life.

LIVING IN New York City with her dog, Tammy was always on the lookout for interesting new places they could go for a walk.

One weekend she left the city to take her dog on a hike in the Berkshire Mountains. Tammy was fascinated by her dog's reaction.

"City dogs spend so much time in unnatural spaces," she says. "It's a wonder when you take them out of the world of cement and just let them experience the environment."

Tammy started Blue Sky Dogs, a service that organizes trips to wilderness areas and beaches within a short drive of New York City. At first her idea was to take dogs on these adventures and then return them at the end of the day to their owners. Quickly she realized that the owners were in need of adventure too, so Blue Sky Dogs was soon organizing outings for both dogs and owners.

Tammy pays close attention to the experiences of dogs and their people. For instance, knowing that the dogs' interest will be focused on all the smells, Tammy brings along a nature expert to tell the owners about the setting they are walking through.

"Most of the people I've taken on these trips would never go by themselves," she says. "They actually first think of it as something good to do for their dog, and then realize they would enjoy it too."

With a dog in our home, we are 16 percent less likely to fall into patterns of compulsive behavior such as excessive computer use or television viewing. (Smith and Esnayra 2003)

44

One Dog, Many Happy People

Many things that make some people happy are irrelevant to others, or even make them unhappy. But dogs contribute to the happiness of everyone around them.

LIKE THE OWNER of any business, Adam is enthusiastic about ideas that might make his employees happier and more productive.

But when Adam, who runs an architectural firm, first thought about dogs in the workplace, he had no idea that a burgeoning group of consulting firms was pushing the idea and a growing list of companies had embraced it as a way to make employees happier. Instead, his assistant asked him if she could bring in her dog for one day while her apartment was being painted.

Adam said yes, thinking that would be the end of it.

But when he noticed the number of people who brightened when they saw a Pekinese sitting beside his assistant's desk, he wondered what would happen if he created a dog welcoming policy.

And the answer, he found out, was that the office became a warmer place to be.

"People's days seem to go a little easier," Adam says. "They're just in a good mood with their dog by their side."

And besides the good feeling in the workplace, there's a direct business benefit as well.

"Not having to worry about getting home for their dog means it's easier to stay late as deadlines approach."

Families with a dog are 18 percent more likely to say that members of the household are generally happy. (Albert and Anderson 1997)

45

Dogs Can Tell Us Things

On the surface, it might seem hard to communicate with dogs. After all, we can't sit down and have a two-way conversation with them. But in their sounds, their body language, and the look in their eye, dogs are constantly communicating with us. Dogs communicate far better with us than we consciously realize.

DOGS EMPLOY SEVERAL different tactics to get a message across. There's tail wagging, running, jumping, barking, and tugging. Scraps is a licker.

Scraps licks to say he likes you. He licks to say he's sorry. Or to say he's hungry. Or to say he wants to go out.

"We think he may be the world champion at licking," says Scraps's owner, Dan. Over the years, between trips to the bathroom to dry off their arms, Dan and his family have become students of licking.

"As far as I can tell, a long repeated licking is a sign of affection," Dan says. "A few courtesy licks is an apology. Anything in between takes some interpretation."

What amazes Dan is how successful Scraps seems to be in getting his message across.

"You can pretty much tell from his reaction if you've figured things out right. And it sure seems like we're getting the gist of it."

In a recent study, dogs and cats were shown the location of a hidden treat they could not access. When a human entered the room, scientists found that dogs were five times more likely to successfully lead the human to uncover the treat than were cats. (Miklósi et al. 2005)

46

Dogs Can Reach Those No One Else Can

It is natural to assume that no creature can connect better with a human than another human. But the truth is that dogs can transcend barriers we often put in place with other humans. And dogs can exhibit a profound joy for life and a joy for the moment, even if that moment is nothing more than getting their ears scratched.

A HEALTH SCIENCE researcher at Oklahoma State University, Sherril doesn't have any interest in fads. She wants hard evidence to support findings about the best ways to help the nursing home patients she studies. And the evidence is clear: dogs help people.

With her team of dogs—Pistol, Pete, Patience, and Patches—Sherril sees what happens when vulnerable humans and dogs are brought together.

"There is an incredible bond that forms," Sherril says. "These are people whose health and frailties have often left them on the outside of life looking in. And then these dogs come in, and they don't care about the wheelchair or the oxygen tank. They don't care what people look like. They are just happy to be with someone."

The positive psychological and physical effects of dogs are so clear that the questions researchers ask are changing. "We're past 'is there an effect?'" says Sherril, "and now we've moved on to 'how big is the effect?'"

Comparisons of recurring nursing home visits by volunteers with a dog and volunteers without a dog showed a 45 percent greater improvement in mood among those visited by a dog. (Lutwack-Bloom, Wijewickrama, and Smith 2005)

47

Dogs Can Teach Us to Be Less Aggressive

A great deal of our lives is a competition. We want to get ahead. We want to show that we're better. But our dogs have no interest in our jealousies or rivalries. Our dogs just want to share affection with us—and that's how they teach us the possibility of seeing others as something more than the competition.

DARYL IS A DOG TRAINER who specializes in helping people teach their first lessons to their new puppies. It's kind of like preschool for dogs.

While puppies are too young to learn some of the more elaborate things an older dog can master, Daryl says that it's still the perfect time to socialize a puppy.

"You should take your puppy absolutely everywhere you can," she says. "Expose your puppy to as many other dogs and people as possible."

Daryl recommends frequent trips to a busy park, where a puppy is sure to meet other dogs and is also likely to attract the admiring attention of many people.

Daryl says that puppies that grow up with a wide social experience tend to become adult dogs that see meeting strangers as something to look forward to. "A dog who has met a lot of people wants to meet even more people, just like that one person you know who gets along with everybody."

In studies of elementary school students, 39 percent of students were rated as less aggressive with their classmates after sessions with a classroom dog. (Sprinkle 2005)

48

Our Relationship with Our Dog Is Unique

We imagine that our relationships with those we are closest to are unlike close relationships anyone else has. Not that others aren't close to their loved ones or don't enjoy each other, but it's not exactly the same as what we have. That's also how it is with our dog. Our connection may look like millions of others, but in truth no one's connection with their dog is quite like ours.

SIX YEARS AGO, when Heidi brought home a new puppy named Muffin, her life was infused with a lot of energy and a lot of mayhem.

Whatever Heidi did, Muffin thought it was a very exciting game of some sort.

When Heidi got out her notebooks and attempted to do some work from home, Muffin would nudge under her elbow and try to climb on her work.

When Heidi did laundry, Muffin would try to dive into the basket.

While other dogs might have tried to chase down squirrels, Muffin ran after them only to try to get them to play with her.

There was a lot of getting used to each other, but even through the trials of getting across basic rules and housebreaking, Heidi was overwhelmed by how cute and loving Muffin was.

When Heidi came in the front door, seeing Muffin race from the back of the house, flopping and slipping until she made it to Heidi, just warmed her heart.

Muffin may be more mannered now, and she's too big to fit in the laundry basket, but she and Heidi still share that feeling of being two great friends.

"I've basically known Muffin her entire life," Heidi says. "It seems like we were made for each other."

Scientists studying people in parks with their dogs identified idiosyncratic play patterns that varied between people and dogs, and even between the same person with multiple dogs. (Mitchell and Thompson 1990)

Dogs Lower Our Blood Pressure

Dogs are such an important source of emotional comfort that they actually affect our physical processes. In fact, spending time with a dog makes it easier for our bodies to function.

DON'S IS A LIFE of deadlines and cranky people. An accountant who runs his own one-man operation, Don has a calendar that revolves around monthly and quarterly tasks and a crushing workload leading up to April 15.

"An accountant is not unlike a dentist," Don says. "You don't want to see us, but you have to. I try to make it as painless as possible for my clients."

In what would otherwise be a workday free of friendly faces, Don can count on Polly to cheer him through the day.

"It's nice to have someone on your side while you're working," Don says. "I can reach down and pat Polly on the head, and feel a little positive energy."

If Don runs into a complex problem, he saves it to think about while taking Polly for a lunchtime walk. "Polly doesn't seem to have the answers, but being outside with her makes it all seem less overwhelming to try to figure them out."

Contact with a dog lowers our blood pressure by 6 percent. (Odendaal 2001)

Dogs Help Us See Past the Surface

What if you could see in people more than is immediately visible on the surface? What if other people could see you in more than a superficial light? Dogs help us do this by distracting us from the trivial things we'd otherwise pay attention to, like what people are wearing, and giving us a chance to connect with other people based on something more substantial.

DONNA HAS AMPLE opportunity to get a sense of some people without even meeting them. As a pet sitter and dog walker, she has access to their homes when they are not there. She knows their schedules. She even takes their mail in.

But Donna doesn't think there's much to be learned from those things.

Donna visits her clients' homes when they are at work or out of town. She feeds, walks, and otherwise takes care of their dogs.

"Of course, I can see their taste in furniture. I can see whether they leave the house sloppy or not," Donna says. "But I'm not a big believer that that tells me anything important.

"Seeing a well-cared-for dog is really about all I need to know about a person," she says. "If they have that, I have them pegged as a pretty good person all around, even if they do leave their socks on the floor."

The clothing of strangers is two times more important in determining whether we think they are friendly if they don't have a dog with them than if they do. (McNicholas and Collis 2000)

51

Dogs and People Were Born for Each Other

From the earliest stages of life, humans and dogs gravitate to each other. Puppies seek human attention, and children seek the affections of dogs. This relationship requires no training, no inducements. It is simply the natural outcome of our species' connection to each other.

WHEN KAREN'S Lhasa Apso jumps into bed with her, there is a reason she doesn't give it a second thought.

"That's our evolutionary relationship right there," says Karen, a biologist.

When the dog-human relationship began, close sleeping arrangements benefited both. "They both helped provide warmth for each other and security for each other. A dog was like a night watchman, alert to any potential threat. And for the dog, being close to humans meant a less dangerous, less exposed sleeping space."

While we no longer share our caves with dogs, Karen said the basic relationship remains intact. "Our appreciation for each other is deeper than humans finding dogs cute or dogs finding us a good source of biscuits," she says. "If humans with dogs and dogs with humans increased their odds of survival living together instead of apart, then we are the living descendants of those who figured that out."

Scientists have found that children, even before they can speak, have a natural affinity for dogs and an ability to communicate with them nonverbally. (Prothmann et al. 2005)

52

Curiosity Didn't Kill the Dog

Unlike cats, for whom this warning was penned, dogs live a life of curiosity. Every smell, every sound, every path is a world of possibility for a dog. Dogs give us a good example of how to approach life—asking, "What's this?" instead of, "What now?"

"IF I NEVER called her inside, I think she would go from blade to blade until she had sniffed the entire front yard," Felicia says of her dog Banjo.

Beyond the smells of the yard, Banjo, a basset hound, can find something of interest wherever she goes.

"She loves car rides. She gets all excited whenever I say the word," Felicia says. "And when we stop, she practically bursts waiting to get out, even when she has no idea where we are."

Even closets are a source of entertainment. "Banjo is transfixed by shoes. She can spend minutes picking out just the right one." Fortunately, Banjo isn't a chewer—she just likes to pick things up and move them someplace else.

An elementary school teacher, Felicia tells her students about Banjo's adventures and says that Banjo's behavior reflects the way humans learn best. "The best learning comes when you let yourself be excited by things," she tells them. "Let yourself wonder and be fascinated."

When people in one study were asked to interpret a dog's expression based on a photo, "curiosity" was the most common answer. (Bahlig-Pieren and Turner 1999)

53

Families with Dogs Are Closer

Growing up with a dog gives us and our families more than a common commitment or even a common source of exercise. It's an experience that also makes us more likely to treat each other well because everyone's worth is assumed, not challenged, and love is not likely to be rationed but available in abundance.

THERE ISN'T A LOT that a youngest child who's a boy in a family of four sisters as much as fifteen years older than him has in common with his siblings.

"When I was in kindergarten, I had a sister in fourth grade, one in middle school, one in high school, and one living on her own," Brian says. "Our lives were very different from each other's. What they were thinking about, what they cared about, what was going on in their lives, was so different from mine, it's like we came from different worlds."

But decades later, Brian can remember one thing that everybody agreed upon: Sniffles was the best dog in the world.

"Even with a big family, it's not hard to feel alone when you have such different lives. But taking care of Sniffles, taking her for a walk, just sitting down with Sniffles by your side, was something we all did, and something we even did together at times," Brian says.

Even after a lifetime of appreciating dogs, Brian still marvels at the fact that it was Sniffles more than any other member of his family who made him feel bound to his sisters when he was young.

People who grew up with a dog in the home were 6 percent more likely to say that their family upbringing was loving. (Vidovic and Vlahovic-Stetic 1999)

54

Dogs Help Us Maintain Mobility

While we are not quite herded like sheep, dogs push us to stay on our feet. Whether by taking walks or moving about in the backyard, dog owners capitalize on the demands of their dogs to stay active for a far longer portion of their lives.

ROBERT RICE IS A gerontologist—a scientist who tries to understand the lives and well-being of older people. Much of what he's learned comes down to a decidedly plainspoken piece of wisdom: "Use it or lose it."

In other words, the biggest difference between those who maintain physical and mental health the longest and those who deteriorate is how much they demand of themselves.

"The biggest danger for older folks is not asking too much of themselves—it's asking too little," Robert says. "When you start looking for ways to avoid challenges, you really begin losing the capacity to remain vital."

There is a long list of activities that Robert encourages people to engage in so that they will be able to stay at the top of their game, and one of them is to have a dog in their lives.

"Dogs help both physically and mentally because paying attention to them, thinking about their needs, and meeting their needs is fundamentally a positive and active task," Robert says. "And the more positive and active the tasks you take on, the longer you will be able to take on whatever you choose."

Dog owners are 25 percent more likely to remain independently mobile into their eighties than nondog owners. (Enders-Slegers 2000)

55

Dogs Help Explain Our Dreams

Dreams can be a window into thoughts we might otherwise be unable to access. Dogs appear in our dreams and often trigger associations with childhood. Keep track of the dogs in your dreams and the circumstances in which they appear and you will gain a deeper understanding of how you became the person you are today.

FOR THE LONGEST time, Aaron would wake up thinking he'd had a notable dream, only to forget all about it by later the same day. He started keeping a notebook by his bed to write down the details of his dreams as soon as he woke up. This helped him discover several interesting patterns, including the fact that his dog Sampson was often in his dreams.

In a recurring dream, Aaron is running, frightened, from an unfamiliar house. As he gets farther away, he begins to fear that he's left Sampson behind. As he stops to go back, he sees Sampson ahead of him, waiting for him.

To Aaron, the dream is a reminder of how central the relationships of his life are—with his wife, his daughter, and his dog. "If I'd left Sampson behind, then escaping from whatever frightened me wouldn't be worth it, because what are we unless we stand up for each other?"

At times Aaron wakes up to see Sampson himself obviously in the throes of a dream. "His feet will move as if he's running, and I can't help but wonder if he's having the same dream."

Dogs frequently appear in the dreams of 52 percent of dog owners. (Doidge 2005)

56

Dogs Help Us Communicate with People

It sounds odd to say that a creature that communicates with barking and body language can have a profound effect on human communication. By providing a common point of reference and concern, however, dogs help us to feel a connection to other humans. That connection makes us feel more comfortable communicating with other people.

PETE HAD NEVER been very successful meeting women. "It was always hard for me to make small talk," he says. "Do we have anything in common? Maybe, but what could it possibly be?"

Soon after moving to Washington, D.C., he spotted something that changed his attitude.

Walking his Labrador retriever Sam through his new neighborhood, Pete stumbled upon a place that just looked very friendly. Stretched across the restaurant's sidewalk patio were dozens of men and women—and their dogs. It turned out that "Doggy Happy Hour" was a tradition at this restaurant.

"It was just the greatest thing," Pete says. "Here men and women automatically had something in common. The conversations were just waiting to happen."

And from an initial meeting, he found that it was easy to come up with a plan for a first date. "You go on a really long walk," Pete says.

"By the time you are done, the four of you are exhausted, and you really know a lot about each other."

The presence of a dog reduces by 45 percent the time it takes before people meeting someone new feel comfortable talking with each other. (Greenbaum 2006)

57

There's Less to Worry About

At any given moment, in any given situation, anyone can think of an almost endless list of subjects that will upset, trouble, or worry them. But dogs make us less likely to focus on those things that undermine our feelings of security. By both offering us comfort and placing demands on our attention, dogs leave us with less opportunity to concentrate on what troubles us.

AS A TEENAGER undergoing chemotherapy, Emily had no shortage of fears and no shortage of pain. Sometimes hospitalized for months at a time, she was often unable to leave her bed.

But there was one completely bright spot in her routine: a visit from Honey, a three-year-old golden retriever. Emily's New York hospital was one of an increasing number that feature visits from pet therapy dogs to help patients feel more comfortable.

Emily's mother, Clare, says there were days when her daughter was so weak that she could barely speak. But when she did, it was about Honey. "This was the only thing that raised her spirits when she was sick," Clare says. "And she was sick constantly."

Emily loved to give Honey a rub on her belly or stroke her thick coat.

With her cancer now in remission, Emily returns to the hospital occasionally for checkups. And every time she goes, she looks to see if

Honey is around. "Honey saved the day for me," Emily says. "When I was with her, I wasn't thinking about chemotherapy at all."

In a study of patients undergoing treatment for the effects of traumatic events, the presence of a dog reduced the likelihood of experiencing high levels of anxiety by 28 percent. (Lefkowitz 2005)

58

We're More Open

Dogs are curious creatures, always searching for something—whether it's food or companionship or the answer to the question "Who peed on this fire hydrant?" With their adventurous and inquisitive spirit, dogs draw out our attention—not only to themselves but to everything around us. Having a dog makes it hard to withdraw from the world.

PENNY HAD THE USUAL list of requirements when she was searching for a new home for her family. It had to be in their price range. It had to have enough bedrooms and bathrooms. It had to have a lot of windows. And one more thing. It had to be in a dog-friendly town.

"Cosmo likes to explore," Penny said of her Labrador retriever. "We all want to get outside and exercise and play together. And we like to take him on long walks and go in different directions. Not just the same route night after night."

Penny says there are a surprising number of communities that make it hard for a dog and a person to enjoy themselves outside.

"Some places have parks that are completely off limits to dogs," she says. "Others can be walled off by streets that are too busy to get around, which kind of cages you into your neighborhood or your block even.

"It's really a very strange situation," Penny says. "Because ultimately the dog-friendly place is the people-friendly place."

People with a dog were 14 percent more likely to be curious about nature and their environment. (Katsinas 2000)

59

Dogs Help Us Resolve Disagreements

A great danger in a family disagreement is that hurtful words will be said in the passion of the moment—words that do not reflect true feelings. Neutral subjects that can prevent us from falling into even deeper disagreement are tremendously useful. This is where our dog comes in, providing a crucial symbol of our shared concerns and a living diversion from our disputes.

TO NADINE, NOTHING seems so absurd as arguing in front of your dog.

"As far as your dog can see, you are a good person, a responsible person, a provider and caretaker. And there you are carrying on about some trivial disagreement."

When tensions rise in her household, Nadine likes to imagine what it looks like from the perspective of Shadow, her Boston terrier.

"If you see yourself towering over your dog, making dramatic gestures and looking ridiculous," she says, "it can really get you to stop and think."

While by no means immune from disagreements over everything from household chores to her mother-in-law, Nadine tries very hard to keep disagreements calm.

"You don't do yourself any good by getting worked up. The calmer you are, the better able you will be to express your basic concerns without getting out of hand."

For Nadine, stopping to pet Shadow in the midst of an argument has proved very helpful. "It's calming, and a good reminder that there are always more things we agree about than disagree about."

Researchers studying household conversations found that the presence of dogs allowed speakers to shift attention away from potential disagreements, reducing the length of disagreements by 17 percent. (Tannen 2004)

60

We See Good Behavior as the Nature of Dogs

One of the ways in which we maintain a positive assessment of ourselves is to think that the good things that happen are caused by our abilities and the bad things that happen are caused by forces out of our control. It's a perspective that heightens our good feelings and softens our bad feelings. We apply the same logic to dogs. We tend to see their good behavior as a function of their personality and their bad behavior as a consequence of a circumstance beyond their control.

RICK BRUNLEY THINKS you can learn a lot about people, and what they think about dogs, when you find out what they named their dog.

Rick, a psychologist who has studied the effects of dogs on people's lives, makes a lot of the fact that the most popular dog name is Buddy.

"Literally, that is the essence of how we conceive of a dog. They are our buddies—reliable, loyal, friendly. Someone we want to have around now and in the future."

Max is also a very popular name. "In Latin, it means 'the great one,'" Rick notes.

Beyond Max, common human names like Charlie and Molly are becoming more popular for dogs. "A few generations ago, it would have been a bit unusual for a family to have a Charlie in the house and have it not be a son. But as dogs become more and more integrated into the life of a family, the name distinctions blur."

As for Rex and Fido, "You don't see that much anymore. Just a few people choose the names because they are common-sounding names that are ironically uncommon.

"People choose very positive names because they have such a good notion of what a dog represents," Rick says.

Observing a group of dogs in a park, nine in ten people explained friendly behavior in a dog as being due to the dog's overall disposition. (Rajecki et al. 1999)

61

Dogs Are Part of the Family

Dogs play such a central role in our lives that they tend to lose their status as pets and gain standing as a family member. And in that role they thrive—never insulting us, complaining, or expressing jealousy, they simply want to be part of a loving family unit.

GLEN HAS HAD dogs in his life as long as he can remember. And whether it was the golden retriever of his youth or the bulldog he shares his home with now, he's always considered his dogs part of the family.

"Take a dog into your life, and you will be astounded at how quickly they fit themselves into your home and into your family," Glen says.

When he first brought Mack into his home, the dog explored the rooms on the first floor, then the second floor. He had the look of someone who thought this was exactly the home he was supposed to have and it was good to have finally arrived there.

And from that first day, Mack could always be found with Glen, his wife, or their two daughters. "He always wants to be with me," Glen says. "I'm not so sure that's true of my human family, but Mack will seek you out."

Like any other family member, there are challenges. The other members of his family are far less likely to dig up the flowers or try to get Glen to throw some of his dinner under the table, but Glen takes that all in stride.

"The ideal family member isn't someone who does exactly what you want them to do all the time," he says. "The ideal family member is supportive and caring and considerate of the other family members, regardless of whether they like to dig up flowers."

For seven out of ten people with a dog, the dog is viewed as a family member rather than as a pet. (Greenebaum 2004)

62

We Have the Same Effect on Each Other

It is always a treat to be in the presence of those whose company we enjoy. But being in the presence of those with whom we feel the closest, strongest connection is not only a joy for us but an obvious joy for them as well. Nothing is stronger than a relationship that runs in both directions—as our relationship with our dog does.

JERRY AND HIS Irish setter Red have been together since Red was a puppy. They're inseparable when Jerry is home, and they both enjoy jogging through the park or playing fetch. Even when Jerry is just watching a game on TV, Red sits right next to him.

Jerry is an airline pilot, and his work often takes him away from home for a few days at a time. When he's away, Red stays with Jerry's sister Mary and her family.

While Jerry's sister and his niece and nephew take good care of Red and take her for walks, they can never get her that interested in playing. It's clear that Red's mind is on Jerry's return.

"Her favorite thing to do is wait for Jerry to come back," Mary says. "Red sets herself up by the front window so she can get a look at whoever comes by, and she keeps a close watch on the front door."

When Jerry does get back, Red races over to him and jumps up at him, standing on hind legs to greet him.

"Those two were really made for each other," Mary says.

Just as dogs reduce our stress levels merely by their presence, humans have the same effect on dogs. (Odendaal 2001)

63

We've Been at This for a Long Time

There are bound to be a few frustrating moments when you might feel like you've had to build a human-dog relationship all by yourself. But humans and dogs—from babies and puppies to adults and older dogs—come together out of more than just chance. As species, we have grown together for tens of thousands of years because both species are better off together than on their own.

FOR JASON AND HIS Rottweiler Hercules, housetraining was a bit of an ordeal. Jason had had dogs before, but they had all seemed to know where and when to do their business.

Jason read books and articles and followed the step-by-step instructions. To get Hercules used to going on paper, he spread newspaper in his hallway.

Hercules seemed to understand the part about going in the hallway, but he always missed the paper. Jason tried to get Hercules on a walk schedule so that he would be outside enough that he wouldn't have to go inside. Accidents continued, however.

Finally, Jason hit on bribery. When Hercules went to the bathroom outside, he got a treat.

Very quickly, the system took hold. The accidents stopped, Hercules received a treat, and everybody seemed happy.

It wasn't long before Hercules' expectation for treats started to rise. If Hercules poked his head out the door and considered going to the bathroom, he expected a treat.

Jason didn't give in, but Hercules stood in the kitchen near the cabinet where the treats were kept.

Eventually, Hercules figured out what it meant when Jason rolled his eyes: you're not getting a treat for that.

Still, through the whole effort it struck Jason that he and Hercules were doing a good job of moving toward meeting their mutual self-interests. "It's like we were playing out the same basic arrangement since the first caveman and dog—I'll do something for you, you do something for me, and we'll get along great."

Dogs were domesticated 100,000 years ago—and have been part of humans' lives more than three times as long as cats. (Catanzaro 2003)

64

Walking the Dog Is Better Than Walking the Self

You might think that a particular form of exercise has the same value no matter who you do it with. But it turns out that walking by yourself and walking with your dog are two very different activities. Walking your dog is much more fun and interesting and is more likely to feel enjoyable instead of just a task to accomplish. That means that you'll still be walking your dog regularly long after you would have given up walking by yourself.

"MOST PEOPLE DON'T think of using their pet as a natural resource to improve their health," says Dr. Henry Brennan. "They let their dog out to do its business and that's it. But if you take your dog and walk with her, that's a great way to get physical activity."

More important, Dr. Brennan says, it changes the nature of walking.

"People drop exercise habits at the slightest inconvenience. You start to skip a day or two, and soon you skip every day. When you start walking with your dog, your dog won't let you stop."

Beyond accountability, Dr. Brennan says that a walk with a dog is just more satisfying.

"There's a little voice inside many people that says, 'It's foolish to take a walk when I'm not trying to get anywhere. What's the point?' But if you are out with your dog, you don't have those concerns."

And most important, he says, "It's more fun because you're doing something together and so you'll want to keep going."

Research comparing regular walkers with regular dog-walkers found that the dog-walkers had lower stress levels and were less likely over the long term to develop cardiovascular disease. (Lacey 2004)

65

Dogs Follow Our Cue

We may be afraid of an unfamiliar dog, but it is important to realize that we have a significant influence on the dog's reaction to us. Dogs look for signs of friendliness and signs of threat and respond very differently depending on our behavior.

"LOTS OF PEOPLE are frightened by unfamiliar dogs," says Greg, a dog trainer. "Unfortunately, people who are frightened tend to anger dogs because the human's alarmed behavior is interpreted as a threat."

Greg says that this self-fulfilling prophecy—seeing a dog as a threat and turning the dog into a threat—is an outcome that can be avoided.

When you encounter a strange dog while walking down the street, Greg says, remember that very few dogs are seeking confrontation. "There are dogs that will defend their territory and defend themselves. But it is very rare for a dog to go after someone in an otherwise innocuous situation or in a neutral location," he says.

We should understand the situation from the dog's perspective, Greg adds. "We're a stranger to the dog. We're bigger than the dog, and our intentions are unknown. The faster you make it clear that you are comfortable, the faster the dog will appear comfortable."

Scientists studying dozens of breeds have found that reactions to strangers who approach in a friendly manner—walking at a normal speed, speaking, petting the dog—are consistently treated very differently than strangers who appear threatening by walking slowly and haltingly and looking into the dog's eye without verbal communication. (Vas et al. 2005)

66

How We Treat Dogs Is More Important Than What Breed They Are

Some people think a lot about the traits of different breeds of dog. They think that if they know the breed, they will have a good idea of the personality and temperament of the dog. But the truth is quite different. The single biggest factor in a dog's personality and ability to learn is not who the dog is but how the dog is treated. Two well-loved dogs of different breeds are likely to be far more similar than two dogs of the same breed who have lived very different lives.

DR. SUE RANCURELLO provided veterinary care at an Ohio shelter when one reality of the job got to her.

"The shelter had limited resources," Dr. Rancurello says. "When a dog was judged unlikely to be adopted, because of age or because it didn't have the right temperament, then it was euthanized. I thought we really needed to give those dogs a chance."

Dr. Rancurello helped to found Second Chance Rescue, an adoption service that takes dogs the shelters think will not find a home and places them in foster homes until a permanent home can be found.

With a limited budget and a handful of volunteers, the organization has helped find homes for hundreds of dogs.

Sue remembers a Lhasa Apso named Lola who was deemed unadoptable because she growled once at a person at the shelter. But after a few months in a new environment Lola was a friendly, loving dog.

Sue, as the name of her group suggests, believes strongly in second chances. "Dogs are not unlike people," she says. "It matters very much how you treat them. They deserve a chance to show how they are when they are loved."

Testing dogs' ability to follow a human's lead through an obstacle course revealed that differences between well-cared-for pet dogs versus working dogs were two times larger than differences between breeds. (Pongrácz et al. 2005b)

67

We Don't Feel Alone

Feeling alone compounds every difficulty we encounter. Solutions seem more remote, and being alone itself only adds another problem to our list. A dog provides an ongoing personal connection in our lives that makes us likely to feel not only less lonely but less isolated from others.

IN JOANNE'S HOME, things were just so. There was no clutter. No dust. Her carpeting was so clean that it looked brand-new. Every piece of furniture had been specially chosen to fit the room it was in. With a busy work schedule and a boyfriend, Joanne's rare free time was spent looking for the perfect antiques to fit her spare room.

After she broke up with her boyfriend, however, Joanne began to feel terribly alone. "There were many days when I didn't interact with anyone beyond purely work-related stuff," Joanne says. "You begin to feel like you could just about disappear."

On a weekend drive, Joanne found herself outside an animal shelter.

"I was not a dog person, ever. But I went inside." And there she found Annie, a cocker spaniel.

The transition was hard. "At first it was a constant lint roller effort to pick up hair Annie had shed and to keep Annie off of this chair or out of that room."

But Joanne soon came to accept that her life had changed, and it was better, if less clean. "With Annie, the house doesn't sparkle, but it feels alive. It feels full. It feels much more like a home to me, and I don't feel alone."

Single adults who have a dog are 37 percent less likely to say that they often feel lonely than single adults who don't have a dog. (Collins 2005)

68

Dogs Provide Teaching Moments

Dogs provide tremendous teaching and learning opportunities within a family. Caring for a dog provides a wonderful example of the obligations and rewards of taking responsibility and sharing love.

ALLISON REMEMBERS ONE of the first lessons she taught her children as they began to graduate from crawling to stumbling to walking. "Take it easy on Barney," she told them all the time.

Barney is a collie—with a gentle disposition but no need to serve as a chair for a forty-pound child.

As her children got older, each one was introduced to taking responsibility for some of Barney's needs. The tasks of walking him, feeding him, and making sure his blanket was shaken out regularly were assigned on a rotating basis.

What struck Allison about the experience was how dedicated her children were to the responsibility. "The older children would supervise to make sure the next one in line was doing everything right. But they didn't really have to, because the younger children took their job so seriously."

Allison knows that it was their love for Barney that drove her children's good behavior and that the lesson they seemed to get was that you should dedicate yourself to your loved ones. "I know it wasn't just that they were extraordinarily responsible—because they never really embraced lessons on washing the dishes nearly as much."

Eight out of ten parents incorporate the care of the dog into life lessons. (Tannen 2004)

69

It Turns Out That We Actually Can Teach an Old Dog New Tricks

---

Despite the familiar saying, it's not true that dogs lose the ability to learn new things. Dogs are creatures of habit, to be sure, but they are not so set in their ways that they cannot absorb well-taught lessons.

"THERE'S A DIFFERENCE between not being able to change our ways and not being willing to change our ways," says Marcus. "Lots of people pretend they can't, but really they just don't want to."

Working as a career counselor, Marcus sees people who lack the imagination to be able to see themselves enjoying a new direction in their life. "They can see how it might fail," Marcus says, "and they can see how it might be unpleasant, but they just don't see how it might be satisfying."

But Marcus doesn't accept that view—not with regard to people, and not with regard to dogs either for that matter. "Anyone can make a change when they think it's in their interest. They just have to understand the situation."

Marcus knows that the notion of not teaching an old dog new tricks doesn't literally apply to dogs. Marcus serves as a "foster parent" for an animal shelter that places dogs in homes temporarily until they are adopted.

While many of the dogs Marcus has dealt with were traumatized and not ready for home life when they arrived, they all learned a new way to be.

"Some of these dogs may never have experienced a loving home before. Some of them may never have been taught basic behavioral rules," he says. "But give them a chance to learn a new way, and they take it."

Scientists studying dogs' reactions to learning a new route for returning home from a walk found that age was unrelated to how quickly the dogs learned the route. (Pongrácz et al. 2005b)

70

Our Love for Dogs Never Runs Out

Your life may change in innumerable ways. Your relationships, your career, your goals, your purpose—all may go through dramatic evolutions. Who you are and what you are will be reshaped by your experiences. But your love for dogs isn't going anywhere.

IN HIS SENIOR year in college, Casey adopted Otis from the pound. Otis is a charmer, with big eyes and a distinctive patch of dark fur on the top of his head.

Casey and Otis have been together through school, Casey's first job, Casey quitting his first job to try to make it as a musician, Casey quitting music and taking a second job, and Casey's several promotions.

"Almost everything about my life has changed in the last ten years," Casey says. "Actually, it's changed several times over.

"Otis was the star attraction of my apartment in college. Then he was kind of the mascot of my band. And now he's made a lot of friends at company picnics," Casey says.

"There were times when dog food and cereal were all that I could afford on my shopping budget. And there were times when everything was going my way. The people I see regularly are all different from the people I saw when I was in music, and they were different from the people I saw at college. But either way, through it all, Otis was my pal.

"It's a nice thing," Casey says, "to be able to count on one part of your life no matter what."

Love and attachment to dogs is unrelated to gender or income or age. (Topál et al. 1998)

71

We Need the Doctor Less

There are few more universal desires than for good health. By encouraging good habits such as regular walks and curbing our tendency to inflict stress on our bodies, dogs are a major factor in helping us maintain good health—and with good health we need far less attention from doctors.

THERE HAVE BEEN very few constants in Jim's life, but having a dog is one of them.

"My father's job transferred him a half-dozen times when I was a kid," Jim says. "That meant a half-dozen schools and a half-dozen efforts to fit in and find new friends. It was very hard on everybody, and very hard on me because I was kind of shy. But we had a beagle named Buster with us, and he was crucial. There was always a friend at home, no matter what else was happening."

As an adult, Jim bounced between wanting a new direction and having no direction before he found his calling as a nurse. All through nursing school and then into his new career, a basset hound named Charlie was at his side.

In his work, Jim has seen the paths that lead to good health and to poor health, and he thinks the power of dogs is underappreciated.

"You hear about drinking lots of water or eating your vegetables. And those are good for you, no doubt. But putting more love, affection, exer-

140

cise, and fun in your life is incredibly helpful. And a dog can help you with all of those."

Over a typical five-year period, dog owners need to see their doctors four fewer times than nondog owners. (Richang et al. 2005)

72

Dogs Teach Us to Accept Differences

It is easy to see the differences between any two people. In fact, when they are profoundly different, it can be hard to see anything the two might have in common. Dogs help us look beyond our obvious differences with other people and allow us to be more open with them.

STUDENTS IN THE alternative program in Atlanta have some kind of physical or emotional impairment that has made a traditional classroom setting a very challenging place for them.

Even in a special setting, with fewer classmates and more attention from teachers and school aides, students in the program tend to have difficulty working with each other.

"A lot of these children have a limited sense of self-worth," said Mary Ann, a teacher in the program. "They tend to see other students not as potential friends but as some kind of threat to avoid."

Mary Ann had heard that some schools brought dogs into the classroom, mostly highly trained therapy dogs that could be easily controlled by their handlers. Mary Ann wondered whether her students might benefit not from these trained dogs but more from dogs that needed training.

"I thought a trained dog would be a passive presence in the room," she says. "But a dog in need of training might be able to reach my students and present them with a common goal."

While her idea was unconventional, Mary Ann ultimately received approval to bring in a group of dogs considered by a local shelter to be too hyper to be good candidates for adoption.

Mary Ann and her students worked with the dogs to teach them basic commands and to try to channel their energy into activities like fetching a ball instead of trying to destroy furniture.

The program has worked. Dog "graduates" of the program have gone on to be adopted, and the students are basking in their accomplishment.

"When you have something positive and collective, it really helps the students see themselves and their peers in a better light," Mary Ann says. "There is a much better sense of acceptance of each other when there is a group accomplishment to build from."

In one study, children were 55 percent more likely to interact with those with physical and mental handicaps in the presence of a dog. (Innes 2000)

73

We're More Likely to Follow a Health Plan

Dogs have a variety of positive effects on our daily habits and well-being. Not only does exercising our dog become a part of our life, but so too does keeping up the routine that is necessary to care for a dog. Developing the habit of sticking to beneficial routines makes us much more adaptable and also more capable of following medical or fitness advice.

PHOEBE HAD BATTLED her weight for a long time. She had struggled through diets, through constantly feeling hungry, through constantly feeling exhausted. Eventually she'd lose some weight. But she couldn't sustain the loss, and inevitably she'd fall off the diet and wind up gaining back all the weight, and sometimes more than she had lost.

She did finally make great strides when she made a new commitment to eating sensibly while not starving herself and exercising consistently without trying to kill herself. She credits the success of her new efforts, which have helped her lose forty pounds and not gain them back, to a pair of hyperactive little cocker spaniels named Princess and Ginger.

"They insist on a walk in the morning," Phoebe says. "The first thing I'm doing every day is something healthy."

And neither dog is inclined to skip a walk. "If it's rainy or cold out, I could easily say, 'I'll just wait until tomorrow.' But Princess and Ginger will follow me around, looking up with their big eyes with that pleading expression, 'Is it time? Are we going now?'"

The difference between trying to sustain her new routine by herself and doing it with the help of her two dogs couldn't be more dramatic. "It's hard to stay focused when it's just you," Phoebe admits. "But when you have somebody else to answer to, it's easier and more fun to keep going."

Participants in a study who were trying to follow a fitness and weight loss plan were 12 percent more likely to meet the recommended targets if they had a dog than if they did not have a dog. (Croteau 2004)

74

Dogs Encourage Cohesion

A t any given moment, members of a family can argue about almost anything, from the crucial to the monumentally trivial. But one thing all family members have in common is the dog. A dog represents shared love and shared responsibility and helps to remind everyone how much they have in common even when they're battling over the remote control.

CHERYL IS STUDYING for a degree in animal behavior. One of her research topics is dogs' communication with other dogs.

That's her day job. Cheryl also has the opportunity to study the subject at home: she and her husband care for Jet and Orion, two greyhounds retired from a life of dog racing.

While Orion quickly took to home life, Jet had a more uncomfortable transition.

"I wouldn't say Jet was abused before we brought him home, but he didn't really know love. His life was almost total isolation punctuated by having to run as fast as he could."

When Cheryl first brought him home, Jet would jump at the slightest sound because everything was so unfamiliar to him. He avoided eye contact and cowered when approached.

A few months after arriving, Jet had become the prototype of the family dog. He basked in Cheryl's attention and loved nothing more than to lie up against her on the couch.

Cheryl says that the experience of caring for Jet and Orion has had a major effect on her life at home. "When you see how sad and empty a life without love is, it's a great reminder to show love to your loved ones as much as you can," she says.

Researchers have found that members of families with dogs are 7 percent less likely to behave aggressively toward each other. (Kotrschal and Ortbauer 2003)

Barking Is Not Random

Because wolves, their close genetic cousins, do not really bark, scientists long thought that barking was a not very functional habit for dogs. They thought that barking was an accident that had somehow been caused by human contact and was therefore not innate dog behavior. But a developing understanding of barking shows that it sends messages and is far more coherent than was once thought.

ONE OF THE FACTS of life when you have four dogs is that you are going to hear a lot of barking. For Jody, figuring out the difference between a casual passing-the-time-of-day bark and an I-feel-like-starting-a-rumble bark has been something of a hobby.

"With four dogs, that's four separate barking styles," Jody says. "But with each dog there are several different sounds to their bark. So now there're at least a dozen barks to try to decipher."

Jody has concluded that dogs have a lot in common with people. "Some of their barking is about something they think is important but you might not think is important, like, the mailman is here and we'd like him to leave. But some of their barking, I really think they don't have anything to say, they just like hearing the sound of their own voice."

Sound analysis indicates that barking varies predictably with the situation that a dog is in. (Yin 2002)

Dogs Keep Us to a Schedule

Too much uncertainty in our day increases our anxiety and decreases our efficiency. To meet their daily needs, our dogs impose upon us a basic schedule for feeding and walking. Following that schedule increases our feelings of control and makes us feel more effective in everything else we do.

"FLASH IS WHAT you might call high-maintenance," Sheila says.

Every day at eight, Flash tells Sheila it's time to go out. "He starts by just looking at me, and if I don't react, he leans on the bed to try to get my attention," Sheila says. "If that fails, he jumps up and tries to give me a little lick on the face."

Sheila could tell time by Flash, who wants out no matter what time they went to bed. "You would think that if I let him out really late he would probably sleep a little longer, but it doesn't work that way."

While she could otherwise sleep an extra hour and still make it to work on time, Sheila eventually gave up any hope that Flash would adopt a new wake-up time. Instead, she started to embrace what she considered the extra hour in her day.

After she lets Flash out, Sheila plows through the required reading for a course she's taking. "If I didn't have this time in my day, I'd probably be trying to cram in ten minutes here and there to get it done. This way it's done and I feel much more relaxed about my day."

And what does Flash do after coming back inside? "He goes back to bed," Sheila says.

Dog owners are 27 percent more likely to say that they follow a regular daily schedule. (Enders-Slegers 2000)

77

We're Nicer

Dogs demonstrate the possibility of unconditional love to us—while at the same time presenting us with an ongoing need for kindness and caring. The example of their behavior, and the example of our own, makes us more capable of seeing the good in other people and being sensitive to their needs.

PEOPLE ARE OFTEN a little surprised when they see Mary and her dogs walking down the street. Mary is a small, grandmotherly-looking woman, and her dogs are Doberman pinschers.

"People see a sixty-year-old and a pair of Dobermans, and they immediately think, 'Something is wrong with this picture,'" Mary says. "Sometimes people ask me if I'm taking care of somebody else's dogs. But no, these guys are mine."

Mary's Dobermans, Skipper and Chief, may look intimidating, but Mary says they couldn't be more friendly. "They're intelligent and loving. They're all bark and no bite."

Mary knows that by reputation, or because of their intimidating look, most people think Dobermans are vicious creatures. But you can no more know a dog by its appearance, Mary points out, than you can know a person that way.

"It's a good lesson to understand that these dogs have individual personalities—they're not all the same," Mary says. "You treat them well,

and they tend to treat you very well in return. It's the same with people really."

People who grew up with a dog were 24 percent more likely as adults to display empathy toward other humans as adults. (Vizek-Vidovic et al. 2001)

78

Dogs Anticipate What We Do

Dogs study us very closely. They very much want to understand what we do and when we do it. They want to know how our activities fit together so that they can fit even better into our lives.

CRAIG'S DOG IS named Floyd, but he calls him The Mayor. The nickname is a tribute to Floyd's boundless interest in the comings and goings of the people on the block and to the way Floyd carries himself—as if his arrival during his night walk is the event everyone on the block has been waiting for.

Craig says that The Mayor has a very developed sense of what goes with what—most specifically, which behaviors are going to lead to his walk.

The Mayor gets excited when Craig puts on his sneakers—which he wears for walks—but not when he puts on other shoes. The Mayor knows the difference between Craig turning the page of the book—nothing particularly interesting will happen next—and Craig closing the book—something, some action, will take place now, possibly a walk. The Mayor has made the same calculation with television. Turning the channel conveys nothing of value, but turning off the TV means possibilities are afoot.

"Sometimes I feel like I hold no surprises for The Mayor, he knows me so well," Craig says.

For a few months, researchers had dog-walkers repeatedly make a brief detour just before they reached their home. After the test was over, more than half of the dogs headed in the direction of the detour without prompting from the human. (Kubinyi et al. 2003)

79

There's More Time for Play

Humans reach an age when it seems undignified to simply play, to do something that has no value whatsoever except for being fun. Dogs are not concerned with dignity. Dogs play because it is in their nature. Play is in our nature too, but too often we try to hide from it. Dogs ask us to throw the ball, run around the park with them, play tug-of-war— and in the process they remind us that it's all right to have fun.

JANET AND HER bull terrier Buddy are frequent visitors to the dog park near their home outside St. Louis.

Dogs and their owners can run around in an enclosed field with no need for leashes. Frisbees and tennis balls are thrown and fetched, and dogs and people make new friends.

"Sometimes when you are walking your dog on a leash, you are so concerned with being polite, keeping your dog off other people and dogs and people's flowers that you kind of kill the fun you might otherwise have," Janet says.

"Here dogs can run around and be exactly who they are, and when you see that, you are reminded a little bit of what that feels like.

"For the dogs, it's like your favorite playground when you were a kid," Janet says. "The one where you felt like you wanted to stay there forever."

Observed for twenty minutes in a waiting area with their dogs, 91 percent of people engaged in some playtime with their dog. (Prato-Previde, Fallani, and Valsecchi 2006)

Dogs Help Us Trust

Caring for a dog is a living symbol of trust. Our dog trusts us to provide for his needs, and we trust our dog to accept us without fear or reservation. Trust is at the foundation of all relationships, and seeing it in our lives helps us apply it to other relationships.

JOHN IS A NATURALLY skeptical person. His ten years as a reporter, listening to all manner of stories that fell apart the moment he looked into the facts, did nothing to make him more optimistic about people.

But with Linus, John may have met his match.

"There's something so genuine about dogs," John says. "They'll tell you what they want, and they'll thank you for it. That's two things most people won't do."

And Linus is so trusting. "I like to fake-throw the dog biscuit, have him run off in search of it, maybe do that a couple of times, and then give it to him. And even though he might be a little suspicious that I'm trying to trick him, he still goes for it every time. It's nice to be trusted that way, even if I'm not worthy of it."

John has extracted a lesson from his experience with Linus. "Never trust a person who doesn't like dogs."

People suffering from an emotional trauma are aided by the presence of a dog because they begin to trust others more than twice as quickly. (Johnson 2001)

We Can Provide Comfort

There are few more satisfying feelings than providing comfort. Offering comfort not only helps reduce another's unease but reinforces our belief that we are capable and kind. Whether it's fear of thunderstorms or strangers or noises in the night, dogs need our reassurance. And when we give it, we both benefit.

JENNIFER'S DOG Bailey has enough fears to fill a book on phobias.

"Bailey will jump at noises, cower from people, run from dogs and other animals, and if a plastic bag should happen to blow by in her path she is terrified," Jennifer says.

When something spooks her, Bailey is prone to running behind the couch, dashing into closets, and whimpering.

Jennifer rescued Bailey, an Airedale terrier, from an animal shelter. "When I first saw her, she was shivering in the corner, too frightened to even try to get someone's attention."

While Jennifer suspects that Bailey was mistreated early in her life, Bailey still has a wonderful loving side.

"She's scared by an awful lot, but when I pick her up, she nestles into my arms and starts to calm down. It's an amazing feeling to see her shift from almost a panic to being peaceful. And when she licks my hand, I know she's feeling better."

In a typical day, dog owners offer physical reassurance to their dog by petting, scratching, or holding their dog at least eleven times. (Prato-Previde, Fallani, and Valsecchi 2006)

82

Dogs Use Their Eyes to Lead Us

Dogs understand that looking at something is a necessary precursor to doing something. When dogs want to communicate where something is, they look at us, then look at the object, in rapid succession. It's a form of communication few other animals share with us.

JILL DISCOVERED Sugar's talent for communicating with her eyes purely by accident.

After a walk, Jill would give Sugar a dog biscuit. Sometimes, just to tease, Jill would pretend to forget about the biscuit, or pretend to forget where they were kept.

Sugar, however, did not forget.

Sugar would race into the kitchen and stand under the cabinet where the box was kept. If Jill did not quickly follow her in, Sugar would run back and forth from Jill to the kitchen, staring up at the cabinet.

When Jill arrived in the kitchen, Sugar would turn back and forth between Jill and the cabinet, as if to say, "It's right there! There! Just open the door, you'll see it."

"It's really very sophisticated, when you think about it," Jill says. "Sugar wants to communicate with me and has concluded that my eyes will follow her eyes, and then my thoughts will follow hers, and I'll get the biscuits out. Some people think dogs don't do abstract reasoning, but if Sugar was just fixated on the biscuits instead of trying to communicate with me, she'd just stare at the biscuits. She wouldn't bother turning back to look at me."

After allowing dogs to watch them hide a piece of food, scientists brought the dogs' owners into the room to see if the dogs could tell their owner where to look. Quickly shifting their eyes between their owner and the object was the means dogs used most frequently to get their owner to unveil the food. (Miklósi et al. 2000)

83

We Don't Have to Be in Charge All the Time

A t work and at home, you have a role you are expected to fill all or nearly all the time. But with your dog, you can be in charge without having to confine yourself to a role all the time. Playing with a dog as an equal is an outlet for fun, and stepping out of your role as leader does nothing to diminish your overall standing. In fact, having some fun with your dog strengthens your standing with your dog.

ELLEN KNOWS IT isn't the typical dog owner's top priority, but making time for soccer with her dog Comet is an absolute necessity in her schedule.

Comet likes to knock the ball forward with his nose—around people, dogs, trees, or anything he can find.

Comet discovered the game when some neighborhood kids played soccer in the street near Ellen's house. From time to time the ball would go into Ellen's yard, and Comet would tear after it.

"You would have thought it was a rolling dog biscuit, the way he went after it," Ellen says.

Ellen saw how much fun Comet had, and how disappointed he was when the kids retrieved their ball.

So Ellen bought Comet his own soccer ball.

"He's so full of energy. And it's such fun to just roll the ball out there and watch him chase it and guide it back," she says. "When I take him to the dog park, while most of the other dogs are kind of dumbfounded, he dribbles right by them. I mean, if there was a World Cup team for dogs, I have no doubt Comet would be a starter."

For Ellen, Comet's enjoyment of soccer is an ongoing reminder of the simple joys in life. "He gets such a kick out of playing with the ball, and I get such a kick out of watching him and seeing other people stare in amazement."

After playing with their owners, dogs are more likely to follow behavioral cues. (Rooney 2002)

84

Dogs Help Us Recover

W hen you suffer a medical difficulty, your recovery depends on the care you receive. But it also depends on your state of mind—your willingness to follow instructions, your ability to imagine a hopeful conclusion, and your efforts to find a path through the pain. In each of these areas, a dog helps you remove your thoughts from the trauma and direct yourself toward recovery.

DR. MARIANNE FELICE would be the first to acknowledge that there isn't much that's pleasant about a hospital stay, especially for children.

"Aside from the medical difficulty that brought them here, and the sometimes uncomfortable treatments they have to endure, there is simply the matter that a hospital is an unfamiliar and intimidating place."

Unfortunately, it's clear that this kind of atmosphere is not helpful to healing. "We've designed a place for healing people much like you would build a factory for making cars. You have all the necessary people and all the necessary tools. The difference is, cars don't care if the building is a frightening place, but people do."

That's why Dr. Felice is a proponent of bringing dogs into the hospital. Trained therapy dogs now roam the rooms at UMass Memorial's Children's Medical Center.

Dr. Felice is so grateful for the dogs' visits that she keeps a container of dog biscuits on her desk to thank them for their help. Dr. Felice knows that research backs up the value of dogs in restoring people to health, but the evidence she's seen is even more overwhelming. "Just look at the faces," she says. "Look at the faces of the patients, the parents, the staff. Nothing but wide smiles. That says it all."

The one-year survival rate among those who have suffered a heart attack is 8 percent higher for dog owners. (Friedmann and Thomas 1998)

85

People Are More Likely to Open Up to Us

People with dogs seem more trustworthy—which means that we are more likely to open up and communicate easily with dog owners.

FOR TRICIA, GETTING people to talk to her is a necessity. As a psychologist, she can't be of any use to people who won't communicate with her. In fact, Tricia needs people not only to talk but to express their thoughts, their feelings, their fears.

And that's why Tricia never goes to the office without her dog Grover.

"A patient comes into this office for the first time, they see a desk, a computer, some chairs, diplomas on the wall," Tricia says. "Those things might suggest, 'This person is competent,' but none of them say anything about this person being caring or compassionate or trustworthy. Now, I could tell you those things are true, but what evidence would you have to back that up? But my three-year-old dog can say all that in the glance of an eye."

For most patients, Grover fades into the background once a session begins. For others, Grover is a continual source of comfort as they sift through their feelings.

"A dog says something about you," Tricia says. "It may be superficial, but there's a sense that you have some consideration in you for others. And people need to feel that about each other."

When asked who they would turn to for discussing an important personal issue, researchers have found that people are 10 percent more likely to rely on a friend who has a dog than on a friend who does not. (Wells and Perrine 2001)

86

Dogs Take On Our Personality

Dogs tend to demonstrate aspects of their owner's personality. It may sound absurd to say that the dog of a cardiologist is meticulous, or that the dog of a musician is boisterous. But dogs are such students of us, and their lives are so profoundly shaped by their human companions, that aspects of who we are become aspects of who they are.

CAROL WORKS FROM home writing technical manuals. Living in a remote area of Colorado, she leads a quiet life. Even with three schnauzers, it's quiet.

While there's a daily run and some chasing of squirrels and whatever else they can find, Carol's friends are shocked at how orderly her life with three dogs is.

"They are really very mellow dogs who want nothing more than to lie at my feet while I work at the computer," Carol says. "Dogs will respond to the world you provide them. They want to fit into your life, and they will if you let them."

Carol says that after a long day of work and then some outside time, the four of them are apt to nearly collapse together. "Jake jumps up next to me. Champ puts his head on my foot. And Missy looks to find a way under my arm so that I almost have to pet her. It's hard to imagine we could feel any closer," Carol says.

Observers separately viewing dogs and dog owners were able to match which dog went with which person in 75 percent of cases. (Roth 2005)

87

Dogs Fit into Our Lives from Birth

B efore we can speak, before we can understand language, we are fascinated by dogs. We see them not as a foreign thing but as a creature every bit as natural to our existence as other humans.

AS A PEDIATRICIAN and as a father, nothing fascinates Michael Rivers more than thinking of little children.

"Young children have a pretty developed sense of friend or foe," Michael says. "As we get older, those lines tend to blur, so much so that the vast majority of what we encounter falls into a middle category.

"But for young children there is a very strong reaction to most things. They think, 'This is either something I want to get closer to or something I should run away from.'"

Dogs tend to be firmly in the friend category. "When you're a couple feet tall, most of the world takes place above you. A dog exists down there with you."

Michael thinks that many adults underestimate how important this can be to children. "There is so much in their lives that is unfamiliar, and so much that can be intimidating," he says, adding that this also explains why children fixate on an object like a security blanket they won't sleep without.

"A good relationship with a dog provides not only that sense of security but the benefits of an ongoing friendship."

Within the first year of life, infants follow the gaze of a dog the same way they follow the gaze of a human. (Johnson, Slaughter, and Carey 1998)

88

Dogs Promote Independence

We know of the amazing power of guide dogs to help the disabled live a far more independent life than would be possible without their assistance. But dogs teach lessons that can help anyone recognize their abilities and embrace the possibilities of their life.

TIM WORKS IN a senior center where he deals with a lot of newly retired people. Part of his job is to help them embrace their new life.

"Most of the retirees at first are thrilled by all the time they have on their hands, but then they are quickly overwhelmed by it," Tim says. "They don't know what to do with the time, and it actually starts to become a burden on them."

Tim says that many of the retirees he talks with don't have a sense of what's next. "They see that what they did is over, but what's next hasn't started or doesn't exist."

After surveying the center's users, Tim was surprised to find that one of the more important differences between those who were enjoying their retirement and those who weren't was whether they had a dog.

"The dog owners were far more likely to say that their days were satisfying and full instead of boring and empty."

Tim started a number of programs to take advantage of the positive influence of dogs, including one to encourage seniors to spend some time volunteering at the local animal shelter.

"When people spend time with dogs, it just seems to put them in the right frame of mind," Tim says.

Schoolchildren exposed to a dog in the classroom improved their ability to work alone by 13 percent over a matched group without a dog in the classroom. (Hergovich et al. 2002)

89

Dogs Make Our Immune Systems Stronger

Petting a dog may seem like a very small event in your day—pleasant for the dog, of course, but not terribly significant. Petting your dog, however, affects the functioning of your own body and actually strengthens your body's immune system.

SUSIE HAD ALWAYS liked dogs, and she occasionally dog-sat her son's greyhound, Miles. But with retirement nearing, she wasn't sure it was the right time to bring a dog of her own into her life.

Susie knew the importance of diet and exercise and everything else that's good for your health. But she was amazed when a doctor told her she might want to spend more time with Miles.

"You think of a dog as being nice and friendly," Susie says, "but you don't think of them as wearing lab coats and making you healthy."

Susie's doctor said that people are less likely to get into a heightened state when they're exposed to the calming effect of a dog. An aroused state interferes with the immune system. Thus, staying calm helps the body fight disease more effectively.

Susie decided to get a dog of her own. "This way we can help take care of each other. And I know someone who owes me a lot of dog-sitting if I ever need it."

Scientists tested for levels of disease-fighting antibodies among three groups of people. Each group sat comfortably on a couch; the first group sat alone, the second was given a stuffed toy animal, and the third sat with a dog. Only one group's immune system strengthened as they sat there: the group with the dog. (Charnetski, Riggers, and Brennan 2004)

90

Dogs Keep Our Secrets

Figuring out how we feel and how we should respond to a troubling situation can be difficult, and sometimes it's helpful to articulate our thoughts before we share them with someone else. Dogs provide a safe outlet for us to formulate words for our troubles and see how they sound—knowing that they will never be repeated.

COMPARED TO OTHER people who work in science, Jesse can count on having the most enthusiastic audiences in the business. Jesse works for a science museum: he takes traveling exhibits from the museum to elementary schools and puts on shows and demonstrations for children.

The topics that Jesse focuses on vary with the seasons and with the museum's current exhibits. So Jesse is constantly practicing new presentations.

For his practice sessions, Jesse demonstrates science lessons not to an audience of one hundred nine-year-olds but to his dog Einstein.

"I've never been able to get up and just speak to myself," Jesse says. "It just feels so strange. It's hard to really maintain your focus and try to practice just talking to yourself."

But with Einstein, a mastiff, Jesse has no trouble delving into chemistry, botany, or astronomy.

And the habit took hold. "If there's anything big I have to say, I've probably said it first to Einstein to make sure it's right."

Now engaged to be married, Jesse tried his proposal out first on Einstein. "I think he thought it was a little wordy. He started to lose interest, and I agreed. Short and to the point is how I decided it should be."

Sixty-two percent of dog owners discuss personal details of their lives out loud with their dogs. (Mueller 2003)

91

Dogs Make Us More Human

No progress in life is possible without caring about those around you. Yet there is a very real challenge in caring for people who are distant, or who seem disconnected, or who have failed at caring before. Dogs help remind us of the possibility of connections, which in turn can make us better at dealing with other humans. Dogs remind us of what we're capable of. Kindness to a dog is a step toward kindness to all those around us.

AT THE MASSACHUSETTS state prison in Plymouth, inmates have the opportunity to train dogs to one day assist deaf and physically disabled people.

Inmates in the program have responsibility for their puppies twenty-four hours a day for more than a year until they are trained.

The prisoners first train the dogs to respond to simple commands, such as sitting and rolling over. Then they move on to more advanced tasks, like teaching the dogs how to turn a light switch on and off and to fetch objects for their future owners.

Keith is an inmate serving a ten-year sentence on drug charges. The dog training program is very much a part of what he hopes will be a new life.

"I've made a lot of wrong choices, and I just wanted to make a right one for a change," Keith says.

He thinks the program has affected him profoundly.

"It's changed me a lot," he says. "I've learned patience. I've learned to think of another's needs before my own. I think this will get me ready to deal with society again."

Inmates who were part of a shelter dog training program in prison have a 26 percent lower likelihood of returning to prison in the subsequent two years. (Strimple 2003)

92

Even Bad Things Are Better

Coping with the worst that life has in store for us is never easy or pleasant. But dogs help us. They may provide just a little distraction or a reminder that we're loved—but the challenges we face are a bit lighter with our dog at our side.

LIFE IN SOUTH Florida can be enviable. The winters are warm. The Gulf of Mexico is nearby.

But hurricane season can quickly turn the good life into a nightmare.

For Jim, Hurricane Charley came in and took his roof with it.

Jim slept in a tent, a trailer, and an apartment during an odyssey that stretched on and on as he tried to rebuild his home and reclaim his peaceful life.

"The stress was unbelievable," Jim says. "It was off the charts."

The one source of calm in his life was a beagle named Tilly.

Other than cowering through the storm itself, Tilly registered nary a complaint. "She didn't seem to care where we slept. She didn't get worked up when we moved, and when we moved again, she just followed me along the way."

Jim said the hurricane disrupted so many of his human relationships that Tilly was often the only one available to share his thoughts with.

"One moment you have a house, the next you don't. One moment you have a job, the next you don't," Jim says. "That just tears you up. I'm thankful Tilly was there to be a friend through all that."

Children accompanied by a dog rated the pain they experienced during a medical procedure as 16 percent less than did children without a dog who underwent the same procedure. (Wells 1998)

93

We See Ourselves as More Lovable

The joy we experience from a dog's love for us lies not only in the relationship itself but also in the inescapable message it provides: that we are lovable, and worth loving.

MANY STANDARDS ARE applied to dogs in competitions. The Laramie County Fair rewards dogs for being lovable. The "Lovable Mutt" contest is a celebration not of the finest appearance and training but of the quality that binds people and dogs.

This year's winner was a three-legged dog named Sammie. Before being taken in by her current family, Sammie lost her leg to a gunshot wound intentionally inflicted by her previous owner. After a veterinarian was able to save her life, Sammie wound up in the care of eight-year-old Brooke and her family.

Sammie and Brooke became inseparable. Sammie wobbles a bit when she walks, but she has learned to get around on her own. Brooke takes care of her and pets and rubs her every day. Her grandmother suggested that they enter Sammie in the contest, to honor not only Sammie's amazing will to survive but the wonderful relationship between Sammie and Brooke.

When Brooke and Sammie took home the Lovable Mutt plaque, Brooke told people, "It just feels nice having a really good dog."

Dog owners are 22 percent more likely to see lovable qualities in themselves. (Johnson 2001)

94

Dogs Contribute to Our Identity

There are countless aspects of your life that contribute to your sense of who you are. Some are sources of pride, some are not. Some are within your control, and some are simply facts you must acknowledge. But one positive point of identification is being a dog owner. For most people, having a dog serves as a subtle reminder to themselves that they are considerate, responsible, capable, and loving.

KEEGAN-MICHAEL KEY hosts Animal Planet's *Funniest Animals* show. But his enjoyment of animals is not just something he cooked up for TV.

Keegan's shepherd/husky/collie mix named Levi is a source of constant amusement and love. Keegan adopted Levi from a shelter just outside Detroit and says that his dog is the cutest, fastest, smartest dog around.

"It's a lot easier to see the good in people, including yourself, when you step up and say, 'I'll take responsibility for this creature. I'll make sure he's safe and loved,'" he says.

Keegan sees his experience with Levi as a daily reminder of not only the great connection they have with each other but also the obligation Keegan feels toward other dogs.

Keegan has worked to promote shelter adoptions and raise money for the cause. "There are so many lovely dogs in this world," Keegan says. "If Levi could talk, I'm pretty sure this is exactly what he'd want me to do."

For more than eight in ten people, having a dog contributes to their sense of who they are. (Tannen 2004)

95

No Animal Better Understands Us

Primates are genetically more similar to humans than any other creature. But try to tell a chimpanzee something and you will be hard-pressed to get your message across. Dogs are uniquely attuned to the messages we send. Dogs study humans and have evolved to build social skills that help them understand us and function around us.

JUST OUTSIDE CHICAGO, visitors to Tom's house find Flowers, a big, playful German shepherd who looks ready for a game of fetch. But Flowers spends far more time at work than she does playing in the yard.

When she's on duty as a police dog, Flowers is ready on Tom's command to search for drugs, guns, or even a missing person. Police dogs can search a building more than five times as fast as a human police officer and are more accurate.

"Flowers found a few grams of narcotics hidden under the vehicle identification number plate in the windshield area of a car," Tom says. "I don't think any human would have found that."

Tom explains that the success of a police dog depends on more than a great sense of smell. "None of what they do for us would be possible if it weren't for our ability to interact with each other. Even though the tasks can be very different, Flowers knows what I'm asking of her, and once we start, there's nothing more important to her than finding what we're looking for."

Dogs are 52 percent more likely to follow human cues, such as pointing toward a source of food, than are primates. (Hare and Tomasello 2005)

96

We Appear Friendlier

We make countless subtle judgments when sizing up another person's friendliness. Their expression, their manners, their body language, their words, and their tone all give us clues we use to decide whether this is a person who wants to talk to us. But even beyond the person's traits, we look to their surroundings for clues. The presence of a dog is processed as a sign of caring and openness to others, and with that impression comes a higher level of assumed friendliness.

AT SUSQUEHANNA UNIVERSITY, administrators had long noticed a problem common to colleges and universities: newly arriving students often felt lost in a sea of new people.

The school offered various orientation activities and other kinds of meetings designed to get new students interacting with each other, but administrators could see that students never really felt comfortable in these situations. And students who go too long without making connections to their peers have a much higher dropout rate.

Kathy, a dean at Susquehanna, hit on an idea that she thought might bring students together and put them at ease: dogs. Kathy invited faculty members to bring their dogs to campus for an afternoon outdoor gathering. Just as Kathy suspected, the dogs were a magnet for students, attracting dozens at a time.

Students sat with the dogs, petting them, scratching their ears, rubbing their bellies, and as they did they met classmates and faculty members in a very friendly setting.

Now the dog sessions are an ongoing part of campus life at Susquehanna.

"If there's one thing you learn in this business, it's that you don't have all the answers," Kathy says, "so you try to find out who does. In this case, it's the dogs who have the right answer."

People meeting someone for the first time were 39 percent more likely to rate that person as friendly if they had a dog with them. (Wells and Perrine 2001)

97

Dogs Help Us See Alternatives

One of the great things about dogs is that they are so obviously different from us and yet they can be so close to us. Seeing this paradox in our relationship with our dogs can encourage us to see other things from a different perspective—to believe in the potential for seeing possibilities where none are obvious.

LORI WAS BY no means a dog person. And her daughter was petrified of dogs. In fact, her daughter's fear was so great that Lori and her husband became concerned that she would not be able to enjoy the simple pleasures of walking down the street, playing in the park, or visiting with a friend because she might encounter a dog.

So they decided there was only one way to conquer this fear: they had to get a dog. Abby, a Labradoodle puppy, came into their lives and soon helped Lori's daughter get past her fears. "She loves all dogs now," Lori says. "The plan worked," she added in an understatement.

Then Abby helped get Lori in a movie.

The producers of the movie *Ocean's Twelve* were searching for extras for the film. They were clear that they were looking for people, not pets.

Still, Lori decided to include a photo of Abby when she submitted her information.

Ultimately, Abby and Lori were asked to be in the film, walking down the sidewalk as the camera looked in on a house where Julia Roberts was talking on the phone.

As for not being a dog person, that's in the past now. "When you meet the right dog, it really can change a lot about how you see things," she admits.

Young inmates involved in a dog training program were 46 percent more likely to think they could succeed later in life. (Schwartz 2003)

98

Man's Best Friend Is Not About to Change

Very few animals take a prominent place in our lives the way dogs do. This is not a random outcome—not just bad luck for goats, say. Dogs and humans have adapted to each other in a way that makes their relationship innate. We could not take another animal into our lives and have the same relationship, even if we were to raise it from birth.

RESEARCHERS IN HUNGARY at Eotvos Lorand University have studied the inclinations and abilities of dogs for decades. One particularly powerful demonstration of the unique nature of dogs involved a group of dogs and wolves raised separately in home settings by researchers.

At the age of four months, both the dogs and the wolves were given the opportunity to try to remove a piece of meat from inside a cage. With their caregiver watching, the animals had to pull on a piece of rope to get the meat. Both dogs and wolves quickly figured out how to get the meat.

Later, the same situation was presented, except that this time the rope was anchored to the cage, making it impossible to get the meat. The dogs tried pulling on the rope, but soon stopped to look at their caregiver for help. The wolves ignored their caregiver and pulled unsuccessfully on the rope until they were exhausted.

Of course, both wanted the meat, but even though they were being raised identically, only the dogs thought that the path to getting the meat was to pay attention to what the human was doing.

To research director Vilmos Csyáni, the test's implications are clear. "Dogs are born very motivated to cooperate with and behave like people," he says. "That's why dogs can do things no other animal can do."

Scientists exposing different animals to the same socialization process found that dogs were more communicative and less likely to avoid human contact than other species. (Gácsi et al. 2005)

We Live Longer

Life with a dog provides countless joys, numerous responsibilities, and, of course, a few challenges. There is perhaps no better tribute to all that dogs do for us, however, than this simple fact: people who care for a dog live longer, healthier lives than those who do not.

"I COULD GET lost in a book all day," says Charlotte. "I could really lose track of what time it is and forget to make dinner. And if I have my hands on a good book, I might not leave the house for days."

That is, Charlotte might do those things if it weren't for Brody.

Brody is a great old friend of uncertain breed who's been with Charlotte, a seventy-four-year-old retiree, for years.

Brody is not subtle when it's time for dinner or time for a walk. "He'll tell you just what he wants and when he wants it," Charlotte says. "But he gives my day a rhythm."

"One of the saddest things you see among folks my age is a feeling of being lost," Charlotte says. "Not knowing what to do, or when to do it, or who to do it with. But Brody will give you an answer for all three."

Even beyond that, Charlotte and Brody have a lot in common. "We both like a nice nap in the afternoon," she says.

On average, people who care for dogs live three years longer than people who have never had a dog. (Richang, Na, and Headey 2005)

You Are Needed

There is nothing more debilitating than feeling that we don't matter, that we lack connections to others, that our presence is unnecessary. A dog disputes that notion every day. We are constantly reminded that we are needed not only when we take care of our dogs' basic needs but also when they show us how very much they enjoy us.

ROBIN AND KEVIN visited an animal shelter, hoping to find a dog to adopt. They were curious about why one dog was set off from the rest, near the lobby of the shelter.

Shelter officials said the dog, a beagle–German shepherd mix, required special attention because she was deaf. Robin and Kevin had never heard of a deaf dog, but not being ones to shy away from a challenge, they brought the dog home and named her Marlee, after the deaf actress Marlee Matlin.

While Marlee doesn't have much of a reaction to strange noises, most of her life is normal. "So much of a dog's focus, especially a beagle, is on smell. And as far as we can tell, she can smell everything," Robin says.

While taking care of Marlee is a great joy, Robin and Kevin recognize that it takes a higher level of attention to keep a deaf dog safe.

"With most dogs, you could let them run around in the yard, and if they started to run off you could call them back," Robin says. "With Marlee, you can't do that. You have to be vigilant with her every second.

She can live a basically normal life with us, but she's not equipped to be out there with people she can't hear and cars she can't hear."

But all that extra attention they pay is not without reward. "She is as good-natured a friend as you could ever ask for," Robin says.

Dog owners are 35 percent less likely to say that they sometimes or often feel unneeded. (Odendaal 2001)

Sources

Albert, Alexa, and Marion Anderson. 1997. "Dogs, Cats, and Morale Maintenance: Some Preliminary Data." *Anthrozoos* 10: 121–23.

Alden, Anne. 2004. "Anthropomorphism in *New Yorker* Dog Cartoons Across the Twentieth Century." Ph.D. diss., Alliant International University.

Anderson, Abby. 2005. "The Use of Animals as an Adjunct to Clinical Therapy: A Review of the Literature Addressing Four Research Questions." Ph.D. diss., Argosy University.

Arambasic, Lidija, Gordana Kerestes, Gordana Kuterovac-Jagodic, and Vlasta Vizek-Vidovic. 2000. "The Role of Pet Ownership as a Possible Buffer Variable in Traumatic Experiences." *Studia Psychologica* 42: 135–46.

Bagley, Debra, and Virginia Gonsman. 2005. "Pet Attachment and Personality Type." *Anthrozoos* 18: 28–42.

Bahlig-Pieren, Zana, and Dennis Turner. 1999. "Anthropomorphic Interpretations and Ethological Descriptions of Dog and Cat Behavior by Lay People." *Anthrozoos* 12: 205–10.

Barker, Sandra, Janet Knisely, Nancy McCain, and Al Best. 2005. "Measuring Stress and Immune Response in Health Care Professionals Following Interaction with a Therapy Dog: A Pilot Study." *Psychological Reports* 96: 713–29.

Bierer, Robert. 2001. "The Relationship Between Pet Bonding, Self-esteem, and Empathy in Preadolescents." Ph.D. diss., University of New Mexico.

Blonder, Lee, Charles Smith, C. Ervin Davis, Marilyn Kesler-West, Thomas Garrity, Malcolm Avison, and Anders Andersen. 2004. "Regional Brain Response to Faces of Humans and Dogs." *Cognitive Brain Research* 20: 384–94.

Brown, Shane, and Ryan Rhodes. 2006. "Relationships Among Dog Ownership and Leisure-Time Walking in Western Canadian Adults." *American Journal of Preventive Medicine* 30: 121–36.

Carlsson, Maj, Ingrid Samuelsson, Anna Soponyai, and Quifang Wen. 2001. "The Dog's Tale: Chinese, Hungarian and Swedish Children's Narrative Conventions." *International Journal of Early Years Education* 9: 181–91.

Catanzaro, Thomas. 2003. "Human-Animal Bond and Primary Prevention." *American Behavioral Scientist* 47: 29–30.

Charnetski, Carl, Sandra Riggers, and Francis Brennan. 2004. "Effect of Petting a Dog on Immune System Function." *Psychological Reports* 95: 1087–91.

Collins, Diane. 2005. "Functional, Psychological, and Economic Benefits of Service Dog Partnership." Ph.D. diss., University of Pittsburgh.

Croteau, Karen. 2004. "Strategies Used to Increase Lifestyle Physical Activity in a Pedometer-Based Intervention." *Journal of Allied Health* 33: 278–81.

Dickstein, Sheryl. 1998. "The Effects of the Presence of a Friendly Dog on Anxiety and Rapport Development." Ph.D. diss., Hofstra University.

Doidge, Norman. 2005. "Dreams of Animals." In *Cultural Zoo: Animals in the Human Mind and Its Sublimations,* edited by Salman Akhtar and Vamik Volkan. Madison, Conn.: International Universities Press.

Downey, D'Ann. 2001. "Understanding the Human-Companion Animal Relationship: A Study of Middle-aged Women and Their Companion Animals." Ph.D. diss., Fielding Graduate Institute.

Enders-Slegers, Marie-Jose. 2000. "The Meaning of Companion Animals: Qualitative Analysis of the Life Histories of Elderly Cat and Dog Owners." In *Companion Animals and Us: Exploring the Relationships Between People and Pets,* edited by Anthony Podberscek, Elizabeth Paul, and James Serpell. New York: Cambridge University Press.

Friedmann, Erika, and Sue Thomas. 1998. "Pet Ownership, Social Support, and One-Year Survival After Acute Myocardial Infarction in the Cardiac Arrhythmia Suppression Trial." In *Companion Animals in Human Health,* edited by Cindy Wilson and Dennis Turner. Thousand Oaks, Calif.: Sage Publications.

Gácsi, Márta, Borbala Györi, Ádám Miklósi, Zsofia Virányi, Enikö Kubinyi, József Topál, and Vilmos Csányi. 2005. "Species-Specific Differences and

Similarities in the Behavior of Hand-Raised Dog and Wolf Pups in Social Situations with Humans." *Developmental Psychobiology* 47: 111–22.

Gácsi, Márta, Ádám Miklósi, Orsolya Varga, József Topál, and Vilmos Csányi. 2004. "Are Readers of Our Face Readers of Our Minds? Dogs *(Canis familiaris)* Show Situation-Dependent Recognition of Human's Attention." *Animal Cognition* 7: 144–53.

Glucksman, Myron. 2005. "The Dog's Role in the Analyst's Consulting Room." *Journal of the American Academy of Psychoanalysis and Dynamic Psychiatry* 33: 611–18.

Gosling, Samuel, Virginia Kwan, and Oliver John. 2003. "A Dog's Got Personality: A Cross-Species Comparative Approach to Personality Judgments in Dogs and Humans." *Journal of Personality and Social Psychology* 85: 1161–69.

Greenbaum, Susan. 2006. "Introduction to Working with Animal-Assisted Crisis Response Animal Handler Teams." *International Journal of Emergency Mental Health* 8: 49–64.

Greenebaum, Jessica. 2004. "It's a Dog's Life: Elevating Status from Pet to 'Fur Baby' at Yappy Hour." *Society and Animals* 12: 117–35.

Hare, Brian, and Michael Tomasello. 2005. "Human-like Social Skills in Dogs?" *Trends in Cognitive Sciences* 9: 439–44.

Hergovich, Andreas, Bardia Monshi, Gabriele Semmler, and Verena Zieglmayer. 2002. "The Effects of the Presence of a Dog in the Classroom." *Anthrozoos* 15: 37–50.

Innes, Fiona. 2000. "The Influence of an Animal on Normally Developing Children's Ideas About Helping Children with Disabilities." Ph.D. diss., Purdue University.

Johannson, Eunice. 2000. "Human-Animal Bonding: An Investigation of Attributes." Ph.D. diss., University of Alberta.

Johnson, Catherine. 2001. "Relationships with Animals as a Component of the Healing Process: A Study of Child Abuse Survivors." Ph.D. diss., Union Institute.

Johnson, Susan, Virginia Slaughter, and Susan Carey. 1998. "Whose Gaze Will Infants Follow? The Elicitation of Gaze-Following in Twelve-Month-Olds." *Developmental Science* 1: 233–38.

Katsinas, Rene. 2000. "The Use and Implications of a Canine Companion in a Therapeutic Day Program for Nursing Home Residents with Dementia." *Activities, Adaptation, and Aging* 25: 13–30.

Keil, Carolyn. 1998. "Loneliness, Stress, and Human-Animal Attachment Among Older Adults." In *Companion Animals in Human Health*, edited by Cindy Wilson and Dennis Turner. Thousand Oaks, Calif.: Sage Publications.

Kotrschal, Kurt, and Brita Ortbauer. 2003. "Behavioral Effects of the Presence of a Dog in a Classroom." *Anthrozoos* 16: 147–59.

Kubinyi, Enikö, Ádám Miklósi, József Topál, and Vilmos Csányi. 2003. "Social Mimetic Behavior and Social Anticipation in Dogs: Preliminary Results." *Animal Cognition* 6: 57–63.

Lacey, Annette. 2004. "Effects of Dog Walking, Walking, and Pet Presence on Women's Stress Levels." Ph.D. diss., Chicago School of Professional Psychology.

Lefkowitz, Carin. 2005. "Animal-Assisted Prolonged Exposure: A New Treatment for Survivors of Sexual Assault Suffering with Post-traumatic Stress Disorder." Ph.D. diss., Widener University.

Lutwack-Bloom, Patricia, Rohan Wijewickrama, and Betsy Smith. 2005. "Effects of Pets Versus People Visits with Nursing Home Residents." *Journal of Gerontological Social Work* 44: 137–59.

Markman, Ellen, and Maxim Abelev. 2004. "Word Learning in Dogs?" *Trends in Cognitive Sciences* 8: 479–81.

McNicholas, June, and Glyn Collis. 2000. "Dogs as Catalysts for Social Interaction: Robustness of the Effect." *British Journal of Psychology* 91: 61–70.

Miklósi, Ádám, R. Polgárdi, József Topál, and Vilmos Csányi. 2000. "Intentional Behavior in Dog-Human Communication: An Experimental Analysis of 'Showing' Behavior in the Dog." *Animal Cognition* 3: 159–66.

Miklósi, Ádám, Péter Pongrácz, Gabriella Lakatos, József Topál, Vilmos Csányi. 2005. "A Comparative Study of the Use of Visual Communicative Signals in Interactions Between Dogs *(Canis familiaris)* and Humans and Cats *(Felis catus)* and Humans." *Journal of Comparative Psychology* 119: 179–86.

Miller, Melody, and Dan Lago. 1990. "Observed Pet-Owner In-Home Interactions: Species Differences and Association with the Pet Relationship Scale." *Anthrozoos* 4: 49–54.

Mitchell, Robert, and Nicholas Thompson. 1990. "The Effects of Familiarity on Dog-Human Play." *Anthrozoos* 4: 24–43.

Mueller, Scott. 2003. "Boys of Divorce and Their Dogs: The Role of the Pet Dog in Helping to Manage Some Gender Role Conflict Issues." Ph.D. diss., University of Hartford.

Odendaal, Johannes. 2001. "A Physiological Basis for Animal-Facilitated Psychotherapy." Ph.D. diss., University of Pretoria.

Pongrácz, Peter, Ádám Miklósi, Viktoria Vida, and Vilmos Csányi. 2005a. "The pet dog's ability for learning from a human demonstrator in a detour task is independent from the breed and age." *Applied Animal Behavior Science* 90: 309–323.

Pongrácz, Péter, Csaba Molnar, Ádám Miklósi, and Vilmos Csányi. 2005b. "Human Listeners Are Able to Classify Dog *(Canis familiaris)* Barks Recorded in Different Situations." *Journal of Comparative Psychology* 119: 136–44.

Prato-Previde, Emanuela, Deborah Custance, Caterina Spiezio, and Francesca Sabatini. 2003. "Is the Dog-Human Relationship an Attachment Bond? An Observational Study Using Ainsworth's Strange Situation." *Behavior* 140: 225–54.

Prato-Previde, Emanuela, Gaia Fallani, and Paola Valsecchi. 2006. "Gender Differences in Owners Interacting with Pet Dogs: An Observational Study." *Ethology* 112: 64–73.

Prothmann, Anke, Konstanze Albrecht, Sandra Dietrich, Ulrike Hornfeck, Saskia Stieber, and Christine Ettrich. 2005. "Analysis of Child-Dog Play Behavior in Child Psychiatry." *Anthrozoos* 18: 43–58.

Rajecki, D. W., Jeffrey Rasmussen, Clinton Sanders, Susan Modlin, and Angela Holder. 1999. "Good Dog: Aspects of Humans Causal Attributions for a Companion Animal's Social Behavior." *Society and Animals* 7: 17–34.

Richang, Zheng, Fu Na, and Bruce Headey. 2005. "Pet Dogs' Effects on the Health and Life Satisfaction of Empty Nester's Parents." *Psychological Science* 28: 1297–1300.

Rooney, Nicola. 2002. "An Experimental Study of the Effects of Play upon the Dog-Human Relationship." *Applied Animal Behavior Science* 75: 161–76.

Rossbach, Kelly Ann, and John Wilson. 1992. "Does a Dog's Presence Make a Person Appear More Likable? Two Studies." *Anthrozoos* 5: 40–51.

Roth, Bennett. 2005. "Pets and Psychoanalysis: A Clinical Contribution." *Psychoanalytic Review* 92: 453–67.

Schwartz, Barbara. 2003. "The Use of Animal-Facilitated Therapy in the Rehabilitation of Incarcerated Felons." In *Correctional Psychology: Practice, Programming, and Administration*, edited by Barbara Schwartz. Kingston, N.J.: Civic Research Institute.

Shaffer, Dennis, Scott Krauchunas, Marianna Eddy, and Michael McBeath. 2004. "How Dogs Navigate to Catch Frisbees." *Psychological Science* 15: 437–41.

Siegel, Wendy. 1999. "Does Learning to Train Dogs Reduce the Noncompliant/ Aggressive Classroom Behaviors of Students with Behavior Disorders?" Ph.D. diss., University of New Orleans.

Smith, Mark, and Joan Esnayra. 2003. "Use of a Psychiatric Service Dog." *Psychiatric Services* 54: 110–11.

Sprinkle, Julie. 2005. "Animals, Empathy, and Violence: An Evaluation of a School-Based Violence-Prevention Program in Select South Carolina Elementary and Middle Schools." Ph.D. diss., University of South Carolina.

Strimple, Earl. 2003. "A History of Prison Inmate–Animal Interaction Programs." *American Behavioral Scientist* 47: 70–78.

Stubbs, Carol, and Mark Cook. 1999. "Personality, Anal Character, and Attitudes Toward Dogs." *Psychological Reports* 85: 1089–92.

Tannen, Deborah. 2004. "Talking the Dog: Framing Pets as Interactional Resources in Family Discourse." *Research on Language and Social Interaction* 37: 399–420.

Topál, József, Ádám Miklósi, Vilmos Csányi, and Antal Doka. 1998. "Attachment Behavior in Dogs: A New Application of Ainsworth's Strange Situation Test." *Journal of Comparative Psychology* 112: 219–29.

Vas, Judit, József Topál, Márta Gácsi, Ádám Miklósi, and Vilmos Csányi. 2005. "A Friend or an Enemy? Dogs' Reaction to an Unfamiliar Person Showing Behavioral Cues of Threat and Friendliness at Different Times." *Applied Animal Behavior Science* 94: 99–115.

Vidovic, Vlasta, and Vesna Vlahovic-Stetic. 1999. "Pet Ownership, Type of Pet, and Socio-emotional Development of School Children." *Anthrozoos* 12: 211–17.

Virányi, Zsofia, József Topál, Márta Gácsi, Ádám Miklósi, and Vilmos Csányi. 2004. "Dogs Respond Appropriately to Cues of Humans' Attentional Focus." *Behavioral Processes* 66: 161–72.

Vizek-Vidovic, Vlasta, Lidija Arambasic, Gordana Kerestes, Gordana Kuterovac-Jagodic, and Vesna Vlahovic-Stetic. 2001. "Pet Ownership in Childhood and Socio-emotional Characteristics, Work Values, and Professional Choices in Early Adulthood." *Anthrozoos* 14: 224–31.

Wells, Deborah. 2004. "The Facilitation of Social Interactions by Domestic Dogs." *Anthrozoos* 17: 340–52.

Wells, Marjorie. 1998. "The Effect of Pets on Children's Stress Responses During Medical Procedures." Ph.D. diss., University of Washington.

Wells, Meredith, and Rose Perrine. 2001. "Pets Go to College: The Influence of Pets on Students' Perceptions of Faculty and Their Offices." *Anthrozoos* 14: 161–68.

West, Rebecca, and Robert Young. 2002. "Do Domestic Dogs Show Any Evidence of Being Able to Count?" *Animal Cognition* 5: 183–86.

Yin, Sophia. 2002. "A New Perspective on Barking in Dogs." *Journal of Comparative Psychology* 116: 189–93.

Acknowledgments

My thanks to Gideon Weil and his colleagues at HarperSanFrancisco, and to my agent, Sandy Choron.